CONSIDERING POETRY

THE NEW SCHOOL SERIES
Consulting Editor: R. Stone, M.A., A.Inst.P.
                       Second Master, Manchester Grammar School
General Editor (Arts): B. A. Phythian, M.A., B.Litt.
                       Headmaster, Langley Park School for Boys,
                       Beckenham

Storylines
A teaching anthology of short stories
W. A. Thompson, M.A.

Listen
Dramatic monologues and dialogues in verse
W. A. Thompson, M.A.

Starting-Points
Creative writing for junior forms
G. P. Fox, M.A.
B. A. Phythian, M.A., B.Litt.

Touchstones
A teaching anthology of poetry in five volumes
M. G. Benton, M.A.
P. Benton, M.A.

Wir Lernen Deutsch
Parts One and Two: Pupil's Book, Teacher's Book, Audio Visual Course
    Part Three in preparation
N. Paxton, M.A., Ph.D.
R. J. Brake, M.A., B.Litt.

Creeds and Controversies
A General Studies book on the nature of religious belief
P. F. Miller, M.A.
K. S. Pound, M.A.

Considering Poetry

An Approach to Criticism

Contributors

W. BARTON, M.A.

R. A. COX, M.A.

G. P. FOX, M.A.

P. JEFFERSON, M.A.

P. M. WILSON, B.A.

M. G. BENTON, M.A.

B. W. DERBYSHIRE, M.A.

J. W. D. HIBBERD, M.A.

W. A. THOMPSON, M.A.

Edited by

B. A. PHYTHIAN, M.A., B.LITT.

Headmaster, Langley Park School for Boys, Beckenham

THE ENGLISH UNIVERSITIES PRESS LIMITED

ISBN 0 340 11465 7

First published 1970
Reprinted 1972, 1973

The English Universities Press Ltd
St Paul's House, Warwick Lane, London EC4P 4AH

Printed and bound in Great Britain by
Richard Clay (The Chaucer Press) Ltd, Bungay, Suffolk.

Contents

Preface

This book provides two or three years' material for the study of poetry by students in sixth forms and in places of further education. It is intended to be used as a basis for work in seminars, and although parts of the book can be read privately by the student, we have generally tried to arrange the material (and use a tone of voice) in a way which will provoke responses from members of a group as fully and frequently as possible. We hope that the stimulation, formulation and sharing of such responses will be the teacher's principal aim.

Even so, any book of this kind is in danger of coming between the student and the poetry he is reading; and nothing should do this. We have been aware of this risk, and consequently have tried to throw as much emphasis as possible on the student's personal development as a reader.

The first two chapters in Part One contain basic work, and it will probably be advisable for students to pass from these to Part Two. The remaining chapters in Part One are less central, and their use will depend on the time available or on the ability of the group; perhaps these chapters are best taken periodically during the students' work on Part Two.

Part Two is an anthology in four sections. Sections A and B contain single poems printed without comment: the first of these sections is appropriate to the first year or so; the second is more difficult. In both, poems are printed according to the alphabetical order of their authors. Section C consists of pairs of poems suitable for comparison. Section D is intended to familiarise students with the sort of appreciation question set by some Examining Boards.

B.A.P.

PART ONE

I READING POETRY

A The Purpose of this Chapter

It may be that you are used to reading poetry, either by yourself or as a member of a group. You may feel well equipped to gain all there is to be gained from a particular poem. If so, this chapter will perhaps be of little use to you; nevertheless we hope you will read through it, since you may find that the methods of reading poetry which are suggested are unfamiliar.

Most people at the start of a course which involves a critical study of poetry feel a sense of inadequacy. What do you *do* with a poem? Read it; enjoy it or dislike it; feel something about it. But why dissect it? After all, poetry wasn't written to be torn apart. Commonly there are dark suspicions that an English teacher is 'reading things into a poem'. Sometimes an interpretation of a poem seems to bear only a distant relevance to the words which are on the page.

Before you can learn how to talk or write about poetry with perception and attention to detail, you must ask yourself the question, 'How do you *read* a poem?'. In this first chapter we suggest several ways in which as an individual or as a group member you may read poetry. You will notice that several of these techniques involve work in small groups which should allow you to talk more often and, usually, more freely than you would in a large class; and this reflects our main concern at this stage of the book. All the later chapters, which will give you an insight into the techniques of the poet's craft and which should equip you with a set of critical tools, will be of little value unless you are prepared to think for yourself, to say what you think, and to respond to the poet's invitation to you as an individual. Poetry is not examination fodder. Rather, reading poetry can illuminate things that happen to people and their responses, and can lead to a better understanding of one's own experiences.

B Some Methods of Approach

Different methods of working with poetry are offered in this section. As you use them you should also *evaluate* them. This in itself should help you in determining which method (or methods) you find both enjoyable and revealing.

Method A
When working with the poems printed below, use this method:

1   Before any discussion, write an 'instant reaction' paper for about 15 minutes. Write down your reactions to the poem as they occur to you: don't bother at this stage with an attempt to produce a highly polished piece of writing yourself.
2   Use the notes you have written as a basis for discussion (e.g. a member of the group might read his notes as a starting-point to the discussion: or you may simply find that the notes have been helpful in clarifying your ideas).
3   Now, at greater length and with more concern for organising your ideas, write a second 'reaction' paper in the light of the discussion.

Fire and Ice
Some say the world will end in fire,
Some say in ice.
From what I've tasted of desire
I hold with those who favour fire.
5 But if it had to perish twice,
I think I know enough of hate
To say that for destruction ice
Is also great
And would suffice.
                                        ROBERT FROST

Days
What are days for?
Days are where we live.
They come, they wake us
Time and time over.
5 They are to be happy in:
Where can we live but days?

Ah, solving that question
Brings the priest and the doctor
In their long coats
10 Running over the fields.

PHILIP LARKIN

Method B
We suggest that you paraphrase the next poem in order to compare
your prose version with the poetry; this will help you to recognise
some of the special qualities this poem possesses.

We would not encourage you to *generalise* about the differences
between 'prose' and 'poetry' too readily; rather, concentrate on this
particular poem and consider the questions that follow.

Orchids
They lean over the path
Adder-mouthed,
Swaying close to the face,
Coming out, soft and deceptive,
5 Limp and damp, delicate as a young bird's tongue;
Their fluttery fledgeling lips
Move slowly,
Drawing in the warm air.

And at night,
10 The faint moon falling through whitewashed glass,
The heat going down
So their musky smell comes even stronger,
Drifting down from their mossy cradles:
So many devouring infants!
15 Softly luminescent fingers,
Lips neither dead nor alive,
Loose ghostly mouths
Breathing.

THEODORE ROETHKE

A purely descriptive poem is, perhaps, the easiest to render in prose. What deductions can you make by comparing the length of the original and the paraphrase?

Presumably you found it necessary to expand 'adder-mouthed', and to explain phrases like 'mossy cradles' and 'So many devouring infants!' What does this tell you about the poet's use of language?

The first verse is a single sentence. How many sentences did it take you to paraphrase this part of the poem? What conclusions can you draw from this about the expression of the poem?

The poem is in free verse which, among other things, isolates 'Move slowly' and 'Breathing' on lines by themselves. What is lost by dispensing with the free verse structure?

What else, if anything, is lost by the paraphrase?

Method C
Read the following poem carefully to yourself:

Telephone Conversation
The price seemed reasonable, location
Indifferent. The landlady swore she lived
Off premises. Nothing remained
But self-confession. 'Madam,' I warned,
5 'I hate a wasted journey—I am African.'
Silence. Silenced transmission of
Pressurized good-breeding. Voice, when it came,
Lipstick coated, long gold-rolled
Cigarette-holder pipped. Caught I was, foully.
10 'How dark?' . . . I had not misheard . . . 'Are you light
Or very dark?' Button B. Button A. Stench
Of rancid breath of public hide-and-speak.
Red booth. Red pillar-box. Red double-tiered
Omnibus squelching tar. It *was* real! Shamed
15 By ill-mannered silence, surrender
Pushed dumbfounded to beg simplification.
Considerate she was, varying the emphasis—
'Are you dark? Or very light?' Revelation came.
'You mean—like plain or milk chocolate?'
20 Her assent was clinical, crushing in its light
Impersonality. Rapidly, wave-length adjusted,

I chose. 'West African sepia'—and as afterthought,
'Down in my passport.' Silence for spectroscopic
Flight of fancy, till truthfulness clanged her accent
25 Hard on the mouthpiece. 'WHAT'S THAT?' conceding
'DON'T KNOW WHAT THAT IS.' 'Like brunette.'
'THAT'S DARK, ISN'T IT?' 'Not altogether.
Facially, I am brunette, but madam, you should see
The rest of me.   Palm of my hand, soles of my feet
30 Are a peroxide blonde. Friction, caused—
Foolishly madam—by sitting down, has turned
My bottom raven black—One moment madam!'—sensing
Her receiver rearing on the thunderclap
About my ears—'Madam,' I pleaded, 'wouldn't you rather
35 See for yourself?'

WOLE SOYINKA

We suggest that the group now discusses this poem in the pattern
set out below:

1. *What does the poem convey?*
It is always worthwhile being clear in your own mind about the
'situation' in a poem: it can prevent you from making misjudged
critical comments later.

   In this case, who has telephoned whom?
               where exactly is the speaker?
               why has the speaker decided to phone?
Now, have the poem read aloud as a dialogue, perhaps more than once,
by readers who try to bring out the changes in tone of voice as the
conversation develops. This will need a few minutes' preparation.

   In the light of these semi-dramatisations what do you think are the
feelings of Wole Soyinka at the following points: lines 4–5; lines
11–14; lines 27–32; lines 34–35?

2. *How does the poem work?*
Try to sort out the dominant characteristics of the poem and their
function. For example, you may want to comment on:

   the aptness of a *telephone* conversation for these two people;
   the way in which the two characters are revealed through the
   dialogue;

7

the effect of chocolate and hairdressing images to describe colour;
the absence of regular rhyme and rhythm.

Clarify any lines whose meaning may still be eluding you. Can you explain, for example,

> 'Shamed
> By ill-mannered silence, surrender
> Pushed dumbfounded to beg simplification.'

and

> 'Silence for spectroscopic
> Flight of fancy, till truthfulness clanged her accent
> Hard on the mouthpiece.'?

3. *Does it succeed?*
Reassess the poem: stand back and consider the whole incident that the poem describes.

If the group can take it, it may well be worth asking your best reader to speak the lines again.

Now you are in a position to answer the question, 'Does the poem succeed in making the incident vivid to you?'

Method D
When discussing the next two poems, you should split up into small groups, perhaps four or five people in each. If possible, use separate rooms.

The group itself decides on the 'pattern' of the discussion. (Will you appoint a chairman? Will you use the three headings suggested in *Method C* or would this inhibit you?) The only instruction we would give you is that each group should appoint a recorder who will present a summary of discussion to the rest of the group when it re-assembles.

Storm on the Island
We are prepared: we build our houses squat,
Sink walls in rock and roof them with good slate.
This wizened earth has never troubled us
With hay, so, as you see, there are no stacks
5 Or stooks that can be lost. Nor are there trees
Which might prove company when it blows full
Blast: you know what I mean—leaves and branches

Can raise a tragic chorus in a gale
So that you listen to the thing you fear
10 Forgetting that it pummels your house too.
But there are no trees, no natural shelter.
You might think that the sea is company,
Exploding comfortably down on the cliffs
But no: when it begins, the flung spray hits
15 The very windows, spits like a tame cat
Turned savage. We just sit tight while wind dives
And strafes invisibly. Space is a salvo,
We are bombarded by the empty air.
Strange, it is a huge nothing that we fear.

SEAMUS HEANEY

You could usefully follow up this discussion next time by looking at Ted Hughes's poem on a similar subject:

Wind

This house has been far out at sea all night,
The woods crashing through darkness, the booming hills,
Winds stampeding the fields under the window
Floundering black astride and blinding wet

5 Till day rose; then under an orange sky
The hills had new places, and wind wielded
Blade-light, luminous black and emerald,
Flexing like the lens of a mad eye.

At noon I scaled along the house-side as far as
10 The coal-house door. I dared once to look up—
Through the brunt wind that dented the balls of my eyes
The tent of the hills drummed and strained its guyrope,

The fields quivering, the skyline a grimace,
At any second to bang and vanish with a flap:
15 The wind flung a magpie away and a black-
Back gull bent like an iron bar slowly. The house

9

Rang like some fine green goblet in the note
That any second would shatter it. Now deep
In chairs, in front of the great fire, we grip
20 Our hearts and cannot entertain book, thought,

Or each other. We watch the fire blazing,
And feel the roots of the house move, but sit on,
Seeing the window tremble to come in,
Hearing the stones cry out under the horizons.

TED HUGHES

Follow the same procedure as before. In the course of your talk you
will inevitably compare the two poems and may be able to justify a
preference.

Method E
This method of approach to a poem involves working in pairs. In a
mixed group, it would be useful in the case of this poem to have both
sexes' opinions represented in each pair, if possible.
1 One member of the pair provides a carefully organised essay in
response to the poem.
2 This essay is then given to the other member of the pair who
writes a second paper in reaction to the first.
3 The two essays are either read aloud to the group, or passed
round together outside class-time in preparation for class discussion. If the essays are read aloud, you may well find it useful to
make notes for reference in an ensuing discussion.

Twice Shy
Her scarf *à la* Bardot,
In suede flats for the walk,
She came with me one evening
For air and friendly talk.
5 We crossed the quiet river,
Took the embankment walk.

Traffic holding its breath,
Sky a tense diaphragm:
Dusk hung like a backcloth
10 That shook where a swan swam,
Tremulous as a hawk
Hanging deadly, calm.

A vacuum of need
Collapsed each hunting heart
15 But tremulously we held
As hawk and prey apart,
Preserved classic decorum,
Deployed our talk with art.

Our juvenilia
20 Had taught us both to wait,
Not to publish feeling
And regret it all too late—
Mushroom loves already
Had puffed and burst in hate.

25 So, chary and excited
As a thrush linked on a hawk,
We thrilled to the March twilight
With nervous childish talk:
Still waters running deep
30 Along the embankment walk.

SEAMUS HEANEY

C   General Points for Discussion

The following points are, we feel, worth your discussion at this
stage. However, as you read more poetry, and as you move further
into this book, it may well be that you could return to these questions.
Possibly, some notes on your reactions to the questions and your
group's discussion would help you to define changes in your own views
if you do return to these questions periodically.

1 Must poetry have a 'special' subject matter? Can poems be
written about absolutely anything? (Love; belief; weather;
sport; party politics; an experiment in physics; dustbins.)

If you find you are out of sympathy with the content of a poem—
say a poem glorifying war, or satirising or advocating a particular
religious view—can you still find it good art?

2 The first question we tend to ask about a poem is 'What does it
mean?'. But the word 'meaning' itself requires exploration.
How does the 'meaning' of a lyric (see Glossary) differ from the
'meanings' of a political satire, a narrative poem or a haiku?

Does 'meaning' in any or all of these cases imply more than the
ideas actually stated?

3 In the light of the poetry you have read, do you think poems must
have recognisable shapes and patterns?

How short can a poem be? Shorter than the haiku on page 117?
Can three words be a poem?

4 In your discussions about the poems in this section you may have
decided, or at least implied, that one poem is 'good', another
'bad', or one 'better' than another. What do you mean when you
use the word 'good' of a poem? (For example, do you mean that
you like it, or that you recognise and appreciate in that poem
certain artistic qualities which must be there in 'good'
poetry?) In fact, can you state by what criteria you evaluate a
poem?

Are there any standards applicable to poetry of any period?

5 Do you think the critical analysis of a poem is a valid and worthwhile process?

2 THE TECHNIQUE OF POETRY

It is best to begin with the assumption that the meaning of any poem is the total effect it has upon the reader, who will respond to it intellectually and emotionally according to how the words on the page work upon his knowledge, his feelings, his experience, his personality, and to some extent his mood. This is not to say that any interpretation is as valid as any other, that any kind of subjective statement of the meaning of a poem is acceptable however outrageous it might seem to others. Opinions that are based on knowledge are likely to be sounder than those based on ignorance, so the best critic is likely to be the one who knows the most about poetry—what has been done in the past, what the poet probably intended, how most intelligent people are going to react to the poet's work. A good critic, one likely to make the reading of a poem a more enjoyable and satisfying experience for others, is one who has read plenty of poetry in order to acquire disciplined standards of comparison. You should be prepared right from the start to offer your opinions readily, for unless you do this, you will make little progress. But your ultimate aim should be to give your opinions the weight of as wide an experience of poetry as possible. Assuming you have this discipline based on familiarity with poetry, then it is true that good practical criticism will be sensitive self-expression—an account of your reading of the poem.

Imagery

A Some Preliminary Considerations

Technical terms are a useful shorthand when we wish to refer to something which is complex and difficult to define, but they have their dangers if we accept them and use them without first experiencing that which they describe. You may have used the word *imagery* before, but try for the moment to forget whatever impressions you have of it.

Think about and discuss these questions.

1 What is an image?
2 What is the connection between *image* and *imagination*?

3 What do *simile* and *metaphor* mean? Make up examples. *Personification* is a type of metaphor. What do you understand by it?

4 'The dove is a symbol of peace.' What does this sentence mean?

B Means of Communication

Your discussion will inevitably lead you towards two main conclusions. One is that in speaking and writing we habitually attempt to make ourselves clear by seeking to define or explain something in terms of something else, by an explicit or implicit comparison. That is to say, for the purposes of communicating exactly what we want to say we make use of an area of experience which has no *literal* connection with the substance of the point we have in mind.

The other conclusion is really contained in the word *habitually* above. A non-literal (*figurative*) use of language is something that is very common indeed in everyday conversation. It is not merely an alien mode of expression used by poets and others for special purposes. There is, however, an important difference nearly always between a conversational use of figurative language and the use made of it by a poet. The difference is usually in the degree of self-consciousness. In conversation we tend to use figurative language carelessly, or unwittingly, or in a hackneyed fashion: we are prone to using *clichés*. But a good poet—either by an instinctive sense of what is apt, or by a painstaking search for the right expression—avoids these dangers.

A poet's aim is to communicate, and what he seeks to communicate is the insight that he has into people and the world. Frequently his feelings are so subtle, so special, so new, that he will have difficulty in achieving the communication. Often he himself will not know exactly what it is he is trying to say until he has written the poem, for, like all of us, he finds that ideas of any complexity become ideas only when they are put into words. Moreover, he is concerned not just with exposition, as—say—the journalist is: he wants to make his reader share the experience, to respond to it in the same way as he does. To do this he has to use language which works not merely on the reader's understanding of the dictionary meaning of words: he tries to engage total response by working on the reader's intellect, memory and senses. He seeks to realise—to make real—the experience by awakening the reader's recognition, by recalling that which the reader has experienced, by bringing into play the reader's five senses.

14

(Most images are visual; but quite often poets use comparisons which appeal to the senses of taste, touch, hearing and smell.)

To achieve this quality of response, this participation by the reader in the poem, the poet uses all the technical devices mentioned in this section; but imagery—which constantly becomes inseparable from diction—plays a major role.

C Images at Work

(a) When we undertake a piece of practical criticism we first have to read so as to find out what the poem says, then analyse the means used to say it, and finally say why we think the poem is or is not a success. Learning to read is perhaps the most difficult of these steps, and so there follows a poem you may have often seen before (indeed you may have been compelled to learn it by heart) but which it is possible you have never *read*.

Daffodils

I wander'd lonely as a cloud
  That floats on high o'er vales and hills,
When all at once I saw a crowd,
  A host, of golden daffodils;
5 Beside the lake, beneath the trees,
Fluttering and dancing in the breeze.

Continuous as the stars that shine
  And twinkle on the Milky Way,
They stretch'd in never-ending line
10   Along the margin of a bay:
Ten thousand saw I at a glance,
Tossing their heads in sprightly dance.

The waves beside them danced, but they
  Out-did the sparkling waves in glee:
15 A poet could not but be gay,
  In such a jocund company:
I gazed—and gazed—but little thought
What wealth the show to me had brought:

For oft, when on my couch I lie
20   In vacant or in pensive mood,
They flash upon that inward eye
    Which is the bliss of solitude;
And then my heart with pleasure fills,
And dances with the daffodils.

This poem is interesting for our purpose in that it is explicitly about the recreation of past experience. It seems very simple, and certainly the thought is not complicated, yet there is a tight control over rhyme, movement, diction and imagery. You may not recognise this; if you don't, come back to it when you have worked through this book. For the moment, consider these questions, which are mainly on its imagery.

1 Try to decide everything that the simile in lines 1 and 2 means. Which qualities of such a cloud throw light on what Wordsworth was doing at the time and on the mood he was in?
2 He chooses 'crowd' and 'host' to describe the number, and says the flowers are 'dancing'. What do these images add to our knowledge of Wordsworth's reaction to the daffodils?
3 'Stars that shine and twinkle on the Milky Way' reinforces the idea of vast numbers. Does it add anything to our idea about the nature, the quality of the flowers?
4 'Wealth' (line 18) takes up an idea which may be contained in a word earlier in the poem, which you probably passed over as a straightforward adjective. Which word?
5 What is it in Wordsworth's experience that the image of riches (line 18) refers to?
6 How does the last line give the poem a roundness, a feeling of there being no loose ends?
7 Comment as fully as you can on these words and phrases.
    sparkling (line 14)
    glee (line 14)
    jocund company (line 16)
    vacant (line 20)
    flash (line 21)
    that inward eye (line 21).

8 Finally, write a few sentences summing up the main impression you have of the kind of imagery Wordsworth uses in this poem, and whether you think this contributes to any unity or coherence or orderly movement of ideas that may be present. (Diction and imagery are inextricably combined in this poem, as in most. Don't worry if you find yourself quoting a word which is not technically an image.)

.   .   .

(b) Read the following poem by George Herbert.

The Church-floore

Mark you the floor? that square and speckled stone,
      Which looks so firm and strong,
            Is Patience:
And th' other black and grave, wherewith each one
5   Is checker'd all along,
            Humilitie:
The gentle rising, which on either hand
      Leads to the Choir above
            Is Confidence:
10 But the sweet cement, which in one sure band
      Ties the whole frame, is Love
            And Charity.
      Hither sometimes Sin steals, and stains
      The marble's neat and curious veins:
15 But all is cleansed when the marble weeps.
      Sometimes Death, puffing at the door,
      Blows all the dust about the floor:
But while he thinks to spoil the room, he sweeps.
      Blest be the Architect, whose art
20   Could build so strong in a weak heart.

1 What is the central idea on which the poem rests?
2 Examine the poem to find examples of personification.
3 To whom does 'Architect' (line 19) refer?
4 Check that you have a clear idea what *emblem* or *symbol* means.

.   .   .

(c) The next poem is by John Donne, the best-known of the 'meta-physical' poets. It may seem over-fanciful at first, but the hyperbolic or startling images contain and illustrate a forceful 'argument' and—many people believe—the poem has great tenderness and sincere feeling. Donne is trying to persuade his wife not to grieve at his departure on a fairly long absence from her.

A Valediction: forbidding mourning

As virtuous men pass mildly away,
    And whisper to their souls, to go,
Whilst some of their sad friends do say,
    The breath goes now, and some say, no:

5 So let us melt, and make no noise,
    No tear-floods, nor sigh-tempests move,
T'were profanation of our joys
    To tell the laity our love.

Moving of th' earth brings harms and fears,
10   Men reckon what it did and meant,
But trepidation of the spheres,
    Though greater far, is innocent.

Dull sublunary lovers' love
    (Whose soul is sense) cannot admit
15 Absence, because it doth remove
    Those things which elemented it.

But we by a love, so much refin'd
    That our selves know not what it is,
Inter-assured of the mind,
20   Care less, eyes, lips, and hands to miss.

Our two souls therefore, which are one,
    Though I must go, endure not yet
A breach, but an expansion,
    Like gold to airy thinness beat.

25 If they be two, they are two so
    As stiff twin compasses are two,
Thy soul the fixed foot, makes no show
    To move, but doth, if the other do.

And though it in the centre sit,
30   Yet when the other far doth roam,
It leans, and hearkens after it,
    And grows erect, as that comes home.

Such wilt thou be to me, who must
    Like th' other foot, obliquely run;
35 Thy firmness makes my circle just,
    And makes me end, where I begun.

1 (a) Put into your own words the comparison in the first six
       lines.
  (b) *Why* do 'virtuous men pass mildly away'? What conclusion do
       you reach from this about the quality of the love between
       Donne and his wife? What reinforcement to this conclusion
       is made by 'profanation'?
2 Donne now shifts to another image. Earthquakes are of significance
  to man from an economic and superstitious point-of-view, but
  'trepidation of the spheres' (normal movement of the earth's axis)
  is 'greater' yet 'innocent'.
  (a) Explain 'greater' and 'innocent'.
  (b) How is this comparison between earthquake and 'trepidation
       of the spheres' relevant to Donne's argument, and how does it
       relate to the second stanza?
3 Stanza 4 asserts that 'Dull sublunary lovers' (what is the full impact
  for you of this phrase?) cannot bear ('admit') absence because the
  essence of their love is sensation or sensuality, and absence destroys
  the basic ingredient of the love affair. His marriage is based on a
  more 'refined' love.
  (a) Discuss the implications and associations of 'refined'.
  (b) What image takes up the same idea?
  (c) What is the connection between that image and Donne's love
       for his wife?

4 Then follows one of the best-known images in English literature. The pair of compasses becomes a symbol of their love, and Donne concludes his argument by demonstrating in detail that his illustration is comprehensively apt, thus seeking to give complete validity to his 'argument'. Of course, there is no real argument: the logician would say 'so what?' The poem is rhetoric not reasoning. Donne was too intelligent a man to think he was organising a step-by-step proof. What he is doing is to search for images which convey the intensity of his feeling, and which engage the intellect of his reader (for this is not an easy poem to understand). For many critics, the result of drawing together the incongruous, the hyperbolic and the demanding is a tension which—strangely—communicates the tenderness and delicacy of Donne's love.

Write a detailed paraphrase of the compasses image.

5 Make sure that you understand all the images in the poem, so that you can read it with ease.

6 Finally, and most importantly, read the poem again to see whether you share the views of those critics mentioned above. (Further comment on this poem is given on page 51.)

.   .   .

(d) The next poem, by Andrew Marvell, was written under the influence of the 'metaphysical' group of poets, and has a good deal of power and violence in its imagery.

To his Coy Mistress
Had we but World enough, and Time
This coyness Lady were no crime.
We would sit down, and think which way
To walk, and pass our long Love's Day.
5 Thou by the Indian Ganges' side
Should'st Rubies find: I by the Tide
Of Humber would complain. I would
Love you ten years before the Flood:
And you should if you please refuse
10 Till the Conversion of the Jews.
My vegetable Love should grow
Vaster than Empires, and more slow.
An hundred years should go to praise
Thine Eyes, and on thy Forehead Gaze.

15 Two hundred to adore each Breast:
   But thirty thousand to the rest.
   An age at least to every part,
   And the last Age should show your Heart.
   For Lady you deserve this State;
20 Nor would I love at lower rate.

   But at my back I always hear
   Time's winged Chariot hurrying near:
   And yonder all before us lie
   Deserts of vast Eternity.
25 Thy Beauty shall no more be found;
   Nor in thy marble Vault, shall sound
   My echoing Song: then Worms shall try
   That long preserv'd Virginity:
   And your quaint Honour turn to dust;
30 And into ashes all my Lust.
   The Grave's a fine and private place,
   But none I think do there embrace.

   Now therefore, while the youthful hue
   Sits on thy skin like morning dew
35 And while thy willing Soul transpires
   At every pore with instant Fires,
   Now let us sport us while we may;
   And now, like am'rous birds of prey,
   Rather at once our Time devour,
40 Than languish in his slow-chapt pow'r.
   Let us roll all our Strength, and all
   Our sweetness, up into one Ball:
   And tear our Pleasures with rough strife,
   Thorough the Iron gates of Life.
45 Thus, though we cannot make our Sun
   Stand still, yet we will make him run.

Although our main concern is with imagery, it is important to be aware of the overall movement of the poem. Notice the progression of the argument from the first word or two of each section:

(a) 'Had we . . .' (If it were the case that . . ., then . . .)
(b) 'But . . .' (It is not the case . . .)
(c) 'Now therefore . . .' (In view of this, . . .)

1 Read the first section again, and discuss the extent to which Marvell is being serious.
2 In lines 21–24 the poem offers a contrast.

(a) What is being contrasted with what?
(b) Are the images powerful?
(c) Compare the pace of line 22 with that of line 24.

3 ' . . . then Worms shall try
That long preserv'd Virginity.' (lines 27–28).
This is clearly a macabre picture: a conscious attempt to convey the physical implications of death and burial. But it does more than this. Indirectly, a contrasting and yet matching experience in life is adduced through the image. What is that?
4 Explain the purpose and effect of lines 31 and 32.
Has the poet's attitude changed?
5 Why 'sits' (line 34)?
6 Explain 'transpires with instant Fires' (lines 34–35).
7 Notice these points about the last ten lines:

(a) an increase in pace coming to a climax in line 44;
(b) the juxtaposition of suggestions of strength and violence with the idea of love;
(c) the image in line 42;
(d) 'Iron gates' probably has as one of its meanings the Iron Gates of the Danube, a place where the river rushes through a narrow gorge.

What conclusions do you reach about the meaning underlying this figurative sequence?

.   .   .

(e) **Ode to Autumn**
Season of mists and mellow fruitfulness!
Close bosom-friend of the maturing sun;
Conspiring with him how to load and bless
     With fruit the vines that round the thatch-eaves run;

22

5 To bend with apples the moss'd cottage-trees,
　　And fill all fruit with ripeness to the core;
　　　To swell the gourd, and plump the hazel shells
　　With a sweet kernel; to set budding more,
And still more, later flowers for the bees,
10 Until they think warm days will never cease,
　　For Summer has o'er-brimmed their clammy cells.

　Who hath not seen thee oft amid thy store?
　　Sometimes whoever seeks abroad may find
　Thee sitting careless on a granary floor,
15　Thy hair soft-lifted by the winnowing wind,
　Or on a half-reap'd furrow sound asleep,
　　Drowsed with the fume of poppies, while thy hook
　　　Spares the next swathe and all its twinèd flowers;
　And sometimes like a gleaner thou dost keep
20　Steady thy laden head across a brook;
　　Or by a cider-press, with patient look,
　　　Thou watchest the last oozings hours by hours.

　Where are the songs of Spring? Ay, where are they?
　　Think not of them, thou hast thy music too,—
25 While barrèd clouds bloom the soft-dying day,
　　And touch the stubble-plains with rosy hue;
　Then in a wailful choir the small gnats mourn
　　Among the river sallows, borne aloft
　　　Or sinking as the light wind lives or dies
30 And full-grown lambs loud bleat from hilly bourn;
　　Hedge-crickets sing; and now with treble soft
　　The redbreast whistles from a garden-croft;
　　　And gathering swallows twitter in the skies.

1 The richness of this poem is only partly achieved through
figurative language, and although you are not at this moment
concerned with making a full analysis, it is important to see
something of how the images which occur principally in stanzas 2
and 3 fit into an overall organisation.

23

Discuss these topics, confining yourself to the first stanza:

(a) The means whereby the ideas of richness, plenty (excess?) are achieved.

(b) The part played by detailed, local, picture-making.

Now read stanzas 1 and 2 again, paying special attention to the first line of the second stanza. Have you any observations to make about the poem's organisation when you realise that there is no main verb in stanza one?

2 In stanza 2 Keats draws four figures engaged in typical autumnal pursuits.

(a) What are the four people doing?

(b) What have they in common?

(c) Would it make any difference to the effect if the people were actually working rather than resting?

(d) Do you find these portraits a successful means of communicating the idea of autumn?

(e) What points of similarity and contrast can you find between stanzas 1 and 2?

3 Now read stanza 3 again. You will see that sound or song is its basis. Spring is far away, but autumn has its music as well as spring.

Comment as fully as you can on these words or phrases, some of which involve sound:

(a) 'barrèd clouds bloom the soft dying day'

(b) 'touch'

(c) 'in a wailful choir the small gnats mourn'.

4 What state of mind is the poet in at the end of the poem? Has there been any change since the beginning?

.   .   .

(f) The next poem—by William Blake—illustrates how an image can dominate a piece of verse to the point where nothing is to be taken literally. The poem has an immediate effect of tension and importance, but the question 'What does it mean?' can only be answered by attempting to find out what the symbols stand for. Many critics would say that the question cannot be answered without a knowledge of

Blake's other writings, but it is important that a poem should have at least some independence of its own.

What meaning does the poem have for you?

The Sick Rose
O rose, thou art sick!
The invisible worm
That flies in the night,
In the howling storm,

5 Has found out thy bed
Of crimson joy,
And his dark secret love
Does thy life destroy.

.   .   .

(g) The imagery of Shakespeare's plays is far too large a subject to be dealt with here in anything like a comprehensive manner. We can only look at a few examples of the local life and colour that Shakespeare introduces into his verse. As a final exercise in this section, read these short extracts and say what seems to you important about their imagery.

I have trusted thee, Camillo,
With all the nearest things to my heart, as well
My chamber counsels, wherein, priestlike, thou
Hast cleans'd my bosom: I from thee departed
Thy penitent reformed.

He that hath suffer'd this disorder'd spring
Hath now himself met with the fall of leaf;
The weeds which his broad-spreading leaves did shelter,
That seem'd in eating him to hold him up,
Are pluck'd up root and all . . .

        The hearts
That spaniel'd me at heels, to whom I gave
Their wishes, do discandy, melt their sweets
On blossoming Caesar: and this pine is barked,
That overtopped them all.

. . . and blest are those
Whose blood and judgment are so well comeddled
That they are not a pipe for Fortune's finger
To sound what stop she please. Give me that man
That is not passion's slave, and I will wear him
In my heart's core, ay, in my heart of heart,
As I do thee.

Diction

This section is meant to be read first in the student's own time. It is intended that the group then go through its main points in class, discussing any difficulties or queries arising from it. The questions it contains have either been numbered and indented or else printed in italics, so that they stand out: it is hoped that they will provide useful points of departure and pointers for discussion. Some of them are designed so that they may be set for written work, if required.

A What is Diction?

Poems are made from words. The poet chooses certain words rather than others and places them in a particular order; the words combine with each other to produce an effect on those who read them. It is clear that some study of a poet's choice and use of words is essential if we are to understand the way poetry works.

In its narrowest sense the term 'diction' refers to that which is different in a poet's choice of words: those parts of his vocabulary which are in some way peculiar to him, such as Milton's liking for words derived from Latin, or Shelley's fondness for such words as *aetherial, daedal, aerial*. But in its widest sense the study of a poet's diction means the study of his total choice of words, and the factors that determine that choice, and extends to the effect of his words and the way they work together.

This section is meant to make you think about how and why a poet chooses his words, and also about the way words work in a poem and on the reader.

B Words are not Counters

A useful key to much of what follows is to remember that words are not counters. Their meaning is not and cannot be fixed, as the worth of coin of the realm is agreed and fixed. Of course a basic meaning of most words is very confidently understood and agreed upon by most people—that is the meaning as given in a dictionary definition. But the total meaning (by which is meant effect) is something which cannot be nailed down: it varies, however slightly, each time the word is used. We may take as an example the adjective *courageous*: it has the same basic meaning but a different 'weight' or effect when applied to a newspaper article, a valorous act, or an invalid facing up to his disability.

It is worth remembering that some words have changed their dictionary meanings in the last few centuries. In Shakespeare's time *presently*, *fond* and *quick* were commonly used in the senses of *at once*, *foolish* and *alive*.

Any history of the English language will tell you of the long history of most of our words, their derivation from Old English (Anglo-Saxon) or Old French, or direct from Latin, or the underworld slang of past ages.

Look up the following in 'The Shorter Oxford English Dictionary', or 'The Oxford English Dictionary': gentle, villain, nice, bless, wife, chortle, glamour, paradise, forlorn hope.

However, this change in dictionary meaning is only the most obvious way in which words are not counters. It is not, for our purposes, the most important.

C   Words and their Associations

A dictionary establishes what one might call the core of a word's meaning; but in poetry, as distinct from certain sorts of prose, the *work* which a word does (which is one way of saying its meaning) is more than to get across its dictionary meaning. One way of illustrating this is to make a transcript that preserves the 'prose' sense of a particular poem (see page 5). In his book *Straight and Crooked Thinking*, R. H. Thouless makes an experiment with two lines from Keats's *Eve of St. Agnes* (Stanza XXV):

> Full on this *casement* shone the wintry moon,
> And threw warm *gules* on *Madeline's fair breast*.

The words here printed in italics are those Thouless considers 'emotionally coloured words', and he replaces them with 'neutral ones':

> Full on this window shone the wintry moon,
> Making red marks on Jane's uncoloured chest.

What is the emotional colouring of the five words italicised?
What is lost by the substitution of a 'neutral' word?
What words in the stanza from the same poem quoted on page 50 are emotionally coloured?

As you will see in other sections, rhythm, imagery, rhyme and other devices of sound or sense, are all means which allow the poet to convey his meaning. A poem seeks to do more than impart information, it imparts an attitude, or suggests an emotional response: it seeks the transmission of feeling as well as, or rather than, facts. In a poem the language takes fire: the reader is encouraged to bring a greater awareness to the words, to allow their suggestions and associations to unfold and work on him in a way they might not in a prose context. A word and its associations have been likened to a comet and the long tail it draws behind it.

Below are printed two passages which illustrate what has been said about words in a *poetic* context. You must not jump to conclusions, however, for the two passages are also designed to act as a check to a too easy assumption that poetry and prose are easy things to name, and that there is an inevitable contrast between them. The first is an autobiographical passage from a seventeenth-century meditation.

> The corn was orient and immortal wheat, which never should be reaped, nor was ever sown. I thought it had stood from everlasting to everlasting. The dust and stones of the street were as precious as gold; the gates were at first the end of the world. The green trees when I saw them first through one of the gates transported and ravished me; their sweetness and unusual beauty made my heart to leap, and almost mad with ecstasy, they were such strange and wonderful things. The men! oh, what venerable and reverend creatures did the aged seem! Immortal cherubims! And young men glittering and sparkling angels! and maids strange seraphic pieces of life and beauty! Boys and girls tumbling in the streets were moving jewels: I knew not that they were born or should die. But all things abided eternally as they were in their proper places.
>
> THOMAS TRAHERNE: *Centuries of Meditation*

from Wonder

How like an Angel came I down!
    How bright were all things here!
When first among his works I did appear
    O how their Glory me did crown!
5 The world resembled His ETERNITY,
    In which my soul did walk;
    And everything that I did see
        Did with me talk.

The skies in their magnificence,
10   The lively, lovely air,
Oh how divine, how soft, how sweet, how fair!
The stars did entertain my sense,
And all the works of God, so bright and pure,
So rich and great did seem,
15   As if they ever must endure
In my esteem.

1 Which is the more alive and vivid?
2 Which shows the more imaginative use of language?
3 Is the language of the second more poetic (in the best sense) than that of the first?
4 What is meant by 'poetic' in the third question?

These two passages prompt the question 'What is poetry'?

One possible definition of poetry is that it is words put into a pattern sufficiently marked to distinguish the writing from prose; another that it is distinguished by a heightened use of language. It is perhaps more profitable to forget definitions and start naming particular works. We need not hope to arrive at a satisfactory definition. Yet one important thing that emerges from these two passages is that, as far as the heightened use of language goes, much imaginative prose is near to poetry in the way it works. Traherne's verses show quite a lively and interesting use of language, but his prose sentences surely come more fully to life and are more evocative than his verses.

It is certainly worth remembering that a distinction between poetry and prose is sometimes less useful than one between imaginative literature and that writing which communicates only on the factual level, or one between imaginative writing that works and that which does not.

Try to think of prose writings you know that show a 'poetic' use of language. Name as many as you can. If you are stuck look at the opening pages of Dickens' 'Bleak House' and Hemingway's 'A Farewell to Arms'.

D   Diction at Work

1. Below are printed lines from Shakespeare's *Antony and Cleopatra*. They are the words the Egyptian queen says over the dying Antony,

who has been brought to his miserable end very much as a result of his infatuation and her deceit. Yet the situation is not a simple one of black and white, disgrace and dishonour; for Antony is able to comfort himself that there is a sense in which he is undefeated even in defeat; nor is it necessary to think the Queen insincere in what she says:

> Noblest of men, woo't die?
> Hast thou no care of me, shall I abide
> In this dull world, which in thy absence is
> No better than a sty? O, see, my women:
> The crown o' the earth doth melt. (*Antony dies.*)
>   My lord?
> O, wither'd is the garland of the war,
> The soldier's pole is fall'n: young boys and girls
> Are level now with men: the odds is gone,
> And there is nothing left remarkable
> Beneath the visiting moon.

Much of the effect here depends on the total dramatic context: what the audience have seen and heard happen during the previous two hours; and much of the interest depends on our understanding of Cleopatra's character. So a full comment can only be made by someone who can set these ten lines against the whole play. However, this does not prevent you from making an interesting study of the effect each word has on you.

1 Comment on those words in the first five lines about which you think anything at all useful can be said. ('sty' is an obvious one to start with because it tells you at once how Cleopatra views the world without Antony. 'Dull' can be joined with it, but you should not neglect 'abide' and 'absence'.)

2 What does 'melt' make you think of?

3 Who, in Roman times, were given 'garlands' (not necessarily flowers)? What then is the meaning of 'the garland of the war'?

4 What might the 'pole' be? Something the soldier looked up to and which led him on in the battle? So what associations are lent to Antony?

5 What other pole was common in Elizabethan times, and was garlanded with flowers?

6 Would this be an appropriate image for Antony? (cf. Brutus' words about Antony in *Julius Caesar* 'For he is given/To sports, to wildness, and much company'.)

7 Does the mention of 'young boys and girls' in the next line influence your opinion at all?

8 Could both images be meant at the one time?

9 Is it likely that the pole star is referred to as well or instead?

10 'Visiting'?

11 What associations does the moon have that are appropriate to this context?

12 Is your appreciation (understanding) of this passage increased or decreased by looking at it in detail and discussing it?

13 Is your appreciation of (interest and pleasure in) this passage increased or decreased by looking at it in detail and discussing it?

You have presumably noticed that Cleopatra seems to feel a sense of betrayal as she watches Antony die: he is leaving her—'Hast thou no care of me?' Clearly this is something that calls for comment, though not in such a limited exercise as you have just tackled. What are we to make of it? Is it an example of Cleopatra's self-centredness, even at this extreme moment of her lover's need? At first it might seem so, but a couple of factors may cause us to modify this judgement. First there is Antony's dying speech, which dwells on his former greatness and accepts his death, the outcome of their adventures, almost with equanimity. Cleopatra's words may be seen as a rejoinder to this. More important is the feeling that her dismay at being left behind is a not uncommon reaction among those who must survive the one they loved: it does not seem possible to face life without him—how can he abandon me to this?

Of course you cannot 'prove' any answer to a problem of this sort; but that does not prevent us from each one making up his own mind on the available evidence, and probably reaching some agreement as to the sort of answer which seems likely and those answers which do not carry conviction. A probable answer is that these four lines *are* spoken by someone who is habitually self-centred, but that they are also a natural and very human expression of dismay at being left alone.

This is one of the most important problems facing those who are learning to read poetry: to what extent is there a 'right' answer? Your discussion of 'melt' and 'pole' should help you to think about this. As has already been indicated there can be no 'proof', but we would surely be justified in feeling that any comment such as the following was too crude and too easy—not so much 'wrong' as inadequate and partial:

> 'This speech shows that Cleopatra is thinking first and foremost of herself. She does not think of what the dying man she is supposed to love would like to hear. All that she can see is that she will be left alone without her protector, and this reveals her essential selfishness. Instead of comforting Antony she even upbraids him: "Hast thou no care of me?"'

A closer look at the language will give the lie to much of this comment: 'noblest', 'abide', 'dull', 'sty'. So will the second half of the speech with its uncalculating admiration of all that Antony was.

.   .   .

2. If you found Cleopatra's speech interesting or difficult you may care to talk about this first stanza of a song from *Cymbeline*, sung over the (supposedly) dead body of Imogen.

> Fear no more the heat o' the sun,
>   Nor the furious winter's rages;
> Thou thy worldly task hast done,
>   Home art gone, and ta'en thy wages:
> Golden lads and girls all must,
>   As chimney-sweepers, come to dust.

1 Would the associations called up for a Jacobean by the figure of a 'chimney-sweeper' be the same as those the word calls up for us?
2 What associations does 'dust' have? In what other context does it most memorably occur?
3 What are the (many?) associations of 'golden' when combined with 'lads and girls'?
4 In the third and fourth lines what occupation (i.e. way of life) is suggested by 'task' and 'ta'en thy wages'?
   (Note the Christian overtones of the metaphor—what are they?)
5 What else does 'task' imply?
6 What is the importance of 'home'? What must the world be therefore?
7 In general, what is the view of life and death suggested in the third and fourth lines?

E How Much Meaning?

It is clear from what we have seen so far that a poet makes his words work hard, harder than the same words would commonly work in prose. Or one might just as well say that the reader works harder. He is willing to pick up shades of meaning because he knows he is expected to. Because they are shades it is sometimes difficult to be sure quite how much meaning we are justified in finding in a line, a poem, a play. We aim for objectivity, and there are checks and arguments (though rarely proofs) that can be brought against eccentric readings and theories; but criticism is a rather subjective business, and its difficulty is part of its fascination. Part of its fascination is also that each new reader is in some sense an explorer who must find his own way in the poem; the maps of other men should help, but each new reading is a recreation—the poem works on the individual reader or not at all.

It is perfectly possible for a man to read a poem, and be able to tell you something of its 'prose meaning', without him *reading* it all in this other sense of read: to recreate the poet's experience. But how do you know it is the poet's experience and that you aren't reading meanings into his words? The answer is that you can seldom *know*—unless you discover that the poet has left a prose gloss on his poem, and even he in cold blood and after years may not recollect or be able to put into prose the meanings he packed into his verse in the heat of composition; or he may not care to be conscious of what his subconscious did. You can only be reasonably sure for your own purposes, and this is a matter of judgement, compounded of informed common-sense, intuition and experience. One purpose of this book is to help you develop your judgement, but wide reading of poetry will do much more, provided that it is reading in the second sense.

An important aid to the development of judgement is debate among yourselves: to challenge and argue out one another's ideas. Try it on the following exercise. Below are some comments on one word, 'footworn', in the last stanza but one of *The Eve of St. Agnes* (Stanza XLI). How far can you agree with these comments? Are they perhaps an elaborate leg-pull?

It would be useful to have a copy of *The Eve of St. Agnes* open. The lovers are trying to escape; in trepidation they unbolt and unlock the massy door, in fear lest one of the drunken sleepers should hear them and awake.

By one, and one, the bolts full easy slide:—
The chains lie silent on the footworn stones;—
The key turns, and the door upon its hinges groans.

In most prose and in verse 'footworn' would be no more than a vivid circumstantial detail, giving us a picture of a threshold stone that has been hollowed out by the innumerable feet that have trodden it. In this poem we are justified in gathering more from it. It reminds us of how, when nerves are strained, the eye notes apparently irrelevant details (see how Porphyro idly notes the fringe on the carpet in stanza XXXII). More important is that by emphasising the multitude of feet that have trodden the threshold Keats makes us feel more keenly the situation of the two lovers, so near to escape, yet still barred from taking that decisive step.

Perhaps the function of 'footworn' is more than that. Look at the first two lines of the last stanza:

> And they are gone: aye, ages long ago
> These lovers fled away into the storm.

These lines are absolutely crucial to the meaning of the poem; for the whole story of the two lovers, so actual and immediate till now, is suddenly pushed back from us and placed in time. The way the last stanza works on us can only be decided when you read the whole poem; but surely there is a link with 'footworn' here. When taken in conjunction with the two lines just quoted is not 'footworn' seen as a first hint at a placing in time of the lovers' story? We are momentarily aware of the centuries preceding the night of the poem, centuries when generations of feet worked away at the stone to round it to a hollow. The first two lines of stanza XLII make us abruptly aware of time stretching the other way, between them and us.

Of course we cannot possibly think all this out as we read the poem for the first time. *Does this mean we cannot feel it? Is poetry meant to be read once only, as prose so often is?* Certainly Keats commented on lines of Shakespeare (both in his letters and his copy of the plays) in a way that showed he allowed individual lines to dwell and expand in his mind. *What do you think?*

F Simple and Effective Diction

Some students, learning to like the effort of detailed comment, fall into an unconscious assumption that the densest and most difficult poetry is the best. As soon as the belief is stated openly it looks unconvincing, but it is a by no means uncommon belief. Words do not have to be out of the way to bring associations, nor need they summon up pictures as 'footworn' does. Even the simplest words, when set in context, can have a powerful effect. This can be illustrated from Wordsworth's poetry.

First a single line (preserved by a comment on it in a letter) from the lost first version of *Resolution and Independence*. The poem tells of how Wordsworth, the victim of sudden but extreme depression, is walking alone on the moors. He sees 'A lonely place, a Pond'

> By which an old man *was*, far from all house and home.

It is Wordsworth's comment on this line in his letter that concerns us here: 'not *stood*, not *sat*, but *was*—the figure presented in the most naked simplicity possible'. In other words the poet has considered and rejected more specific and seemingly vivid words in favour of the simple verb 'was', which best, because most baldly, gives us the sense of the man's presence.

In more than one poem Wordsworth quotes with great effect the words of the beggars or the country poor who are the subjects of those poems. In *The Excursion* (Bk. 1) a pedlar tells of how he learnt the sad story of Margaret, a deserted wife. After a long illness her husband was thrown out of work, and hung around the house all day, trying to find occupation, or

> to the town
> Would turn without an errand his slack steps;
> Or wander here and there among the fields.
> One while he would speak lightly of his babes,
> And with a cruel tongue: at other times
> He tossed them with a false unnatural joy:
> And 'twas a rueful thing to see the looks
> Of the poor innocent children. 'Every smile,'
> Said Margaret to me, here beneath these trees,
> 'Made my heart bleed.'

When read in context this brief sentence, the first that we hear Margaret speak, is peculiarly effective.

G   Context

Context helps to decide a word's meaning. Not only do words bring life and meaning to a poem by their associations, they receive life and meaning from the words around them. Their context determines which particular associations and meanings of a word will be received by the reader. To see how a word's 'colour' depends on its context we may look at 'white'. Asked what the associations of 'white' are, you will probably first answer 'innocence', but this is only one significance of the word.

Below are printed several brief extracts which contain the word 'white'. Try to see what meaning the word has in each case and how the context influences its effect.

(a) And then to awake, and the farm, like a wanderer white
    With the dew, come back, the cock on his shoulder: it was all
        Shining, it was Adam and maiden,

              .   .   .

    Nothing I cared, in the lamb white days, that time would take me
    Up to the swallow thronged loft by the shadow of my hand.
             (DYLAN THOMAS' elegy for his childhood: *Fern Hill*)

Is either of these uses *merely* descriptive?

(b) *Her* lips were red, *her* looks were free,
    Her locks were yellow as gold:
    Her skin was white as leprosy.
                (COLERIDGE: *The Ancient Mariner*)

(c) The rose leaves, like flakes of crimson snow,
    Paved the turf and the moss below.
    The lilies were drooping, and white, and wan,
    Like the head and skin of a dying man.
                (SHELLEY: *The Sensitive Plant*)

(d) The One remains, the many change and pass;
    Heaven's light forever shines, Earth's shadows fly;
    Life, like a dome of many-coloured glass,
    Stains the white radiance of Eternity,
  5 Until Death tramples it to fragments.
                (SHELLEY: *Adonais*)

(Shelley is preferring that which is unstained and indivisible—and revealed at Death—to the beautiful but imperfect perceptions of it that are all that we have in this life.)

(e) Henry Vaughan (1621–95) writes, like Dylan Thomas, of lost childhood innocence:

> Happy those early dayes! When I
> Shin'd in my Angel-infancy.
> Before I understood this place
> Appointed for my second race,
> 5 Or taught my soul to fancy ought
> But a white, Celestial thought.

(f) O fat white woman whom nobody loves,
   Why do you walk through the fields in gloves?
                 (FRANCES CORNFORD: *To a Fat Lady seen from a Train*)

(g) Who is the smiling stranger
   With hair as white as gin,
   What is he doing with the children
   And who could have let him in?
                 (CHARLES CAUSLEY: *Innocent's Song*)

(The figure masquerades as Santa Claus but changes to Herod, while the threat of nuclear destruction looms over the poem.)

(h) The following is a complete poem, T. E. HULME's *Autumn*:

> A touch of cold in the Autumn night—
> I walked abroad,
> And saw the ruddy moon lean over a hedge
> Like a red-faced farmer.
> 5 I did not stop to speak, but nodded,
> And round about were the wistful stars
> With white faces like town children.

These quotations should provide material for a discussion of how a single word is capable of suggesting many and very different associations, and of the importance of context.

Before leaving this topic of how words can take on different meanings depending on the context, it is worth remembering this effect in mock-heroic and parody, or when irony is used. Mock-heroic depends for its effect on the use of phrases identical or similar to those used in genuine epic poetry; and parody also must employ the same sort of diction as its model. In the case of irony the context tells us that words which are capable of bearing a certain meaning are in fact to be taken in a quite different sense.

H 'Poetic Diction'

In conclusion we must look at another factor influencing a poet's choice of his words. A poet does not necessarily feel free to use any word at all in the language. At certain periods most writers have agreed that certain words are unfit for poetry, others peculiarly fit. This 'agreement' is sometimes formulated into a recognised theory and is observed by virtually all writers, but sometimes it is quite unconscious and is not everywhere observed.

In the eighteenth century the feeling that some words and phrases are poetic and others are not was particularly strong. Some of you will have already come across Wordsworth's objections to the artificial and dead phrasing of the time, its 'poetic diction'. He expressed his reaction in his prose preface to *Lyrical Ballads*, and in practice in the experimental poems that were printed in that volume. It was his intention to use 'a selection of language really used by men', in contrast to what he considered the frigid and artificial set phrases, the formulae, of so much eighteenth-century writing. In this extract from his Preface (1800) Wordsworth quotes a sonnet by Gray and comments on it:

> 'In vain to me the smiling mornings shine,
> And reddening Phoebus lifts his golden fire:
> The birds in vain their amorous descant join,
> Or chearful fields resume their green attire:
> 5 These ears, alas! for other notes repine;
> *A different object do these eyes require;*
> *My lonely anguish melts no heart but mine;*
> *And in my breast the imperfect joys expire;*

Yet Morning smiles the busy race to cheer,
10 And new-born pleasure brings to happier men;
The fields to all their wanted tribute bear;
To warm their little loves the birds complain.
I fruitless mourn to him that cannot hear
And weep the more because I weep in vain.'

It will easily be perceived that the only part of this Sonnet which is of any value is the lines printed in Italics: it is equally obvious that except in the rhyme, and in the use of the single word 'fruitless' for fruitlessly, which is so far a defect, the language of these lines does in no respect differ from that of prose.

Is there then, it will be asked, no essential difference between the language of prose and metrical composition? I answer that there neither is nor can be any essential difference.

It is worth looking at Gray's sonnet again, and the difference Wordsworth points out between those lines that are printed in italics, and those that are not. To help you consider Wordsworth's comments there are two poems printed below, one by Wordsworth, and one by Hopkins. Their subjects are in some part akin to Gray's, in as much as they deal with the renewal of nature, and the song (or activity) of birds is poignantly felt; but it is interesting to see how the manner and destination of these three poems is so very different.

Lines Written in Early Spring
I heard a thousand blended notes,
While in a grove I sate reclined,
In that sweet mood when pleasant thoughts
Bring sad thoughts to the mind.

5 To her fair works did nature link
The human soul that through me ran;
And much it griev'd my heart to think
What man has made of man.

Through primrose-tufts, in that sweet bower,
10 The periwinkle trail'd its wreathes;
And 'tis my faith that every flower
Enjoys the air it breathes.

The birds around me hopp'd and play'd:
Their thoughts I cannot measure,
15 But the least motion which they made,
It seem'd a thrill of pleasure.

The budding twigs spread out their fan,
To catch the breezy air;
And I must think, do all I can,
20 That there was pleasure there.

If I these thoughts may not prevent,
If such be of my creed the plan,
Have I not reason to lament
What man has made of man?

Spring

Nothing is so beautiful as spring—
  When weeds, in wheels, shoot long and lovely and lush;
  Thrush's eggs look little low heavens, and thrush
Through the echoing timber does so rinse and wring
5 The ear, it strikes like lightnings to hear him sing;
  The glassy peartree leaves and blooms, they brush
  The descending blue; that blue is all in a rush
With richness; the racing lambs too have fair their fling.

What is all this juice and all this joy?
10   A strain of the earth's sweet being in the beginning
In Eden garden.—Have, get, before it cloy,
  Before it cloud, Christ, lord, and sour with sinning,
Innocent mind and Mayday in girl and boy,
  Most, O maid's child, thy choice and worthy the winning.

1 Do you agree with Wordsworth's comment on Gray's sonnet, and
  the relative merits of those lines printed in italics and those that
  are not?
2 How far does Wordsworth's practice in his poem conform to
  those precepts quoted from the Preface?

3 Which words and phrases from the first verse of Wordsworth's poem would seem mannered if used in a modern poem?

4 How far is Hopkins' language that of prose?

5 How effective is the language of each *for its purpose*?

Poetic diction was very marked in the century preceding the publication of the *Lyrical Ballads* (1798). Some of its worst excesses may be seen among those country parsons who wrote on wildly inappropriate, because trivial, subjects in grand Miltonic style. Something of this may be seen in the work of a much more interesting poet, Cowper, as when in the third book of *The Task* he describes in high-flying verse the proper cultivation of cucumbers ('the prickly and green-coated gourd/So grateful to the palate'):

> The stable yields a stercoraceous heap,
> Impregnated with quick fermenting salts,
> And potent to resist the freezing blast.
>
> .   .   .   .   .
>
> Warily, therefore, and with prudent heed,
> He seeks a favour'd spot; that where he builds
> Th' agglomerated pile his frame may front
> The sun's meridian disc.

It is interesting to ask why exactly this seems unsatisfactory. Is it that details of cultivation are not a fit subject for poetry? If so, which other subjects are impossible for verse? Cowper would certainly have been able to reply to any such objection by pointing to a long tradition, including Vergil's *Georgics*. Perhaps the answer lies in the discrepancy between subject and style; and when poetic diction is silly or vicious it is so because of this discrepancy, because manner and meaning are inappropriate to each other. Grand style is a functional style for a grand subject.

It ought to be said that the best eighteenth-century poetry marries subject and style successfully, as, for example, in Johnson's *The Vanity of Human Wishes*.

There is little space to illustrate the different poetic styles of the different centuries and the poetic dictions that form a part of them. Shakespeare's Sonnet 130, *My mistress' eyes are nothing like the sun*, printed on page 51, gives some indication, though in mirror image, of the sentiment and expression of many Elizabethan sonnets; but Shakespeare is deliberately going against the convention, which was to praise the loved one in hyperbolic terms of the precious and rare. Thus Spenser writes (*Amoretti*, Sonnet 15):

> For lo! My love doth in herself contain
> All this world's riches which may far be found—
> If sapphires, lo! her eyes be sapphires plain;
> If rubies, lo! her lips be rubies sound;
> If pearls, her teeth be pearls bothe pure and round.

Here subject, approach and diction all conform to a convention, the convention of service and adoration in love. Just as many poets of the same generation have a similar vocabulary, so their subjects and their approaches to those subjects often show a common concern.

The late eighteenth and early nineteenth century interest in the Gothic (all things medieval and mysterious) influences Keats in *The Eve of St. Agnes*, and this extends to his choice of words: 'all amort', 'I've mickle time to grieve' or 'pleas'd amain'. The same spicing with archaic words to suggest a medieval atmosphere is even more obvious in Coleridge's *The Ancient Mariner*, especially the original version, which is larded with such words as 'Eftsones', 'eldritch', 'Gramercy'. In the 1930's, on the other hand, many poets made a conscious effort to introduce the imagery and vocabulary of an industrial civilisation into their poetry. Thus Louis MacNeice writes:

> The jaded calendar revolves,
> Its nuts need oil, carbon chokes the valves,
> The excess sugar of a diabetic culture
> Rotting the nerve of life and literature.

As you continue to read more widely you will be able to form some idea of the different styles of writing that predominated at different periods. The previous section in this book contains several examples from the Metaphysical poets of the first half of the seventeenth century. The present section quotes two examples of comparatively unsuitable poetic diction from the eighteenth century. Part Two (pages 133 to 209) provides examples from other centuries.

43

Rhythm

This section deals with the special contribution which rhythm makes to the full effect of a poem. When you have worked through this section, you should be equipped to talk and write about rhythm when it seems to you to be important in practical criticism. But first, a word of warning: because a separate section is devoted to it, don't be misled into thinking that rhythm is something apart from the meaning of a poem, or that it is always worth talking about and that it should be treated separately as a subsection of a paragraph on style. If you feel that rhythm has contributed little to your experience of a poem, perhaps because it is trivial in comparison to some other powerful feature that gives the poem point for you, then concentrate on that dominating feature and say little or nothing about rhythm. In fact, this will seldom be the case.

A Some Preliminary Discussion

First, using the questions below, think and talk about rhythm in general without special reference to poetry. This is perhaps best done in small groups. Then exchange the ideas which come up within the groups in a full discussion.

You are not expected to arrive at comprehensive answers to all of these questions, but each of you will probably have something to contribute to your group's understanding of what they entail. Some of the questions may suggest lines of thought that will help you to answer others. Don't aim at dictionary-type definitions where you are asked for meanings; but a good dictionary might prove useful to start the discussion moving again if you get stuck.

1 What do we mean by *chaos*?
2 What do we mean by *order*?
3 Do men in general prefer order to chaos? Evidence?
4 Can we be too orderly?
5 What do we mean by a monotonous arrangement of things?
6 How do we avoid monotony without reverting to chaos?
7 What is the difference between *order* and *symmetry*?

Now treat the next group of questions in the same way.

1 Which of these things have *rhythm* of any kind?
  (*a*) the heart, (*b*) the tides, (*c*) the blood, (*d*) the seasons, (*e*) the flow of gas along a pipe, (*f*) the internal combustion engine, (*g*) a spinning-top, (*h*) air escaping from a punctured tyre, (*i*) life, (*j*) sunlight, (*k*) direction indicators, (*l*) St. Paul's Cathedral (the building).

2 What else besides sounds and movements can be rhythmical?

3 Can rhythm have a soporific effect upon men's minds? Evidence?

4 Can rhythm act as a stimulant? Evidence?

5 If it can be either soporific or stimulating, what makes it one or the other?

6 In what ways do irregularities enhance the rhythmical effect in music and in dance?

7 How far would you say a new pop record is likely to depend for its commercial success on (*a*) the strength, (*b*) the complexity, (*c*) the originality of its rhythm?

B Types of Rhythm

It might now be useful to attempt a classification of those features of language that the poet can make use of for rhythmic effects.

1. Syllable-stress

Words have their own rhythms. These are determined partly by the stresses we always place on certain syllables. Such stresses may be subject to regional variations, but in what is called 'standard English' pronunciation the stresses within words are firmly fixed. We should regard, for instance, a stress placed on the first or third syllable of the word 'occasion' as definitely wrong; such a mispronunciation would suggest that English was not the speaker's native tongue.

2. Emphatic Stress

English has another kind of stress which we lay on whole words within the phrase or sentence. This stress shifts to different words according to the tone of voice the speaker wishes to convey and to the meaning he wants them to carry.

I want *you* to read this book.
I want you to read this book.

I *want* you to read this book.

I want you to read *this* book.

The movement of the emphatic stress radically alters our response to what is said.

The falling of both syllable and emphatic stresses helps to create the rhythms of the language. It would be a bad poet who disregarded these natural rhythms or chose to break the rules affecting them for no good reason.

3. *Phrase or Sentence Movement*

By careful control of the length of phrases within the sentence or the length of sentences within the larger unit of paragraph or stanza, the writer can create various rhythmic effects which will evoke particular responses in the reader or listener. Politicians, preachers and advertising men, for instance, have all demonstrated in their prose the excitatory power of repetition and of the build-up of forceful phrases. But poets too, in a more subtle way perhaps, have made use of the variations in speed and weight that control of the length of phrases can give to the rhythm of their work. Obviously length of phrase will not on its own produce different kinds of verse movement: the sound-effects of the words and the emotive value of their meaning and associations will be in part responsible. But here are a few passages in which the rhythmic movement of the language, regular or irregular as the case may be, helps to suggest a particular mood or scene and evoke a special response in the reader. Discuss what effect each has.

(*a*)   from Morn
     To Noon he fell, from Noon to dewy Eve,
     A Summer's day.
                    (MILTON : *Paradise Lost*)

(*b*)   through many a dark and dreary Vale
     They pass'd, and many a Region dolorous,
     O'er many a Frozen, many a fiery Alp,
     Rocks, Caves, Lakes, Fens, Bogs, Dens, and Shades of Death.
                    (MILTON : *Paradise Lost*)

(c)   Every branch big with it,
          Bent every twig with it;
        Every fork like a white web-foot;
        Every street and pavement mute:
      Some flakes have lost their way, and grope back upward, when
      Meeting those meandering down they turn and descend again. . . .
                              (HARDY: *Snow in the Suburbs*)

(d) He reached down from a fissure in the earth-wall in the gloom
      And trailed his yellow-brown slackness soft-bellied down,
          over the edge of the stone trough
      And rested his throat upon the stone bottom,
      And where the water had dripped from the tap, in a small
          clearness,
      He sipped with his straight mouth,
      Softly drank with his straight gums, into his slack long body,
      Silently!
                              (D. H. LAWRENCE: *Snake*)

(e) One thing that literature would be greatly the better for
      Would be a more restricted employment by authors of
          simile and metaphor.
      Authors of all races, be they Greeks, Romans, Teutons, or
          Celts,
      Can't seem just to say that anything is the thing it is but have
          to go out of their way to say that it is like something else.
                              (OGDEN NASH: *Very Like a Whale*)

4. Metre

The metre of most English poetry is created by the arrangement of
stressed and unstressed syllables in various regular patterns within the
line of verse. Until the twentieth century most English poets used
metre all the time, choosing the metrical form in which they felt most
inspiration or the one best suited to the nature of their subject. You
don't have to be an expert on prosody to be sensitive to the rhythms
created in verse by the metre, but you will find it useful to be able to
recognise some of the common metres of English verse and to know
the jargon for referring to them. Before you go any further, consult

the Glossary (under *Metre*) for definitions of *metrical foot* and the common types—*iambic, trochaic, dactyllic, anapaestic* and *spondaic*. Finally make sure you understand such basic technical terms as *caesura, enjambement* and *elision*.

With this technical knowledge you should have no difficulty in recognising the basic metres of the following extracts. A word of warning here: this is meant as no more than a preliminary exercise in recognition. Obviously, in any sensitive reading of verse, we should only be faintly conscious of the basic metre, forming an unobtrusive framework of rhythms on which a wide variety of other stresses, some lighter, some heavier, often working *against* the basic metre, or following the natural rhythms of the language, is built. The last thing we wish to encourage is a dull-witted 'ke-bonk, ke-bonk' style of reading verse.

(*a*) Music, when soft voices die,
    Vibrates in the memory;
    Odours, when sweet violets sicken,
    Live within the sense they quicken.

(SHELLEY)

(*b*) But at my back I always hear
    Time's winged chariot hurrying near;
    And yonder all before us lie
    Deserts of vast eternity.

(MARVELL: *To His Coy Mistress*)

(What effect does the change in the first foot of the second and last lines have here?)

(*c*) One more Unfortunate,
    Weary of breath,
    Rashly importunate,
    Gone to her death!

    Take her up tenderly,
    Lift her with care,
    Fashion'd so slenderly,
    Young, and so fair!

(HOOD: *The Bridge of Sighs*)

(d) The Assyrian came down like the wolf on the fold,
   And his cohorts were gleaming in purple and gold;
   And the sheen of their spears was like stars on the sea,
   When the blue wave rolls nightly on deep Galilee.

(BYRON: *The Destruction of Sennacherib*)

5. *Verse Forms*

As well as adopting common metres, some poets have chosen to shape
their work into stanzas of conventional design, in which the number of
lines, their metre, the number of syllables they contain and the rhymes
at the end are all fixed by tradition. The more common forms are
described in the Glossary.

Poets have also experimented with stanza form, making all the
properties of metre, line-length and rhyme suit or even suggest in
themselves the shape and movement of their subject. Look, for
instance, at the opening passage of Henry Vaughan's *The Water-fall.*
How far do you think it suggests, by its rhythms, movement and sound-
effects, the water-fall itself?

   With what deep murmurs through time's silent stealth
   Doth thy transparent, cool and watery wealth
         Here flowing fall,
         And chide, and call,
5 As if his liquid, loose Retinue stayed
   Lingering, and were of this steep place afraid,
         The common pass
         Where, clear as glass,
         All must descend
10   Not to an end:
   But quickened by this deep and rocky grave,
   Rise to a longer course more bright and brave.

Of course there is little point in merely identifying the basic metre or
verse form a poet has used. This knowledge is only valuable if it
enables you to say how the poet's rhythms work in evoking or
controlling your feelings, creating tension, making pleasing sound-

patterns—in any way helping you to enjoy the poem by contributing to the special experience it offers. It is likely, in fact, that you will spend more time in discussing the irregularities and departures from the basic forms, for it is often the modifications of the fundamental pattern that enable the poet to produce his most remarkable effects (as you saw in extract (b) of the metre-recognition exercise above).

For practice, pick out the irregularities in the metres of the following passages and show what effects are created by them:

(a) Ay, but to die, and go we know not where;
    To lie in cold obstruction, and to rot;
    This sensible warm motion to become
    A kneaded clod; and the delighted spirit
  5 To bathe in fiery floods, or to reside
    In thrilling region of thick-ribbed ice;
    To be imprison'd in the viewless winds,
    And blown with restless violence round about
    The pendent world; or to be worse than worst
10 Of those that lawless and incertain thoughts
    Imagine howling—'tis too horrible.
    The weariest and most loathed worldly life
    That age, ache, penury, and imprisonment
    Can lay on nature is a paradise
15 To what we fear of death.

(SHAKESPEARE: *Measure for Measure*)

(b) She hurried at his words, beset with fears,
    For there were sleeping dragons all around,
    At glaring watch, perhaps, with ready spears—
    Down the wide stairs a darkling way they found—
  5 In all the house was heard no human sound.
    A chain-droop'd lamp was flickering by each door;
    The arras, rich with horseman, hawk, and hound,
    Flutter'd in the besieging wind's uproar;
    And the long carpets rose along the gusty floor.

(KEATS: *The Eve of St. Agnes*)

(c) My mistress' eyes are nothing like the sun;
    Coral is far more red than her lips' red;
    If snow be white, why then her breasts are dun;
    If hairs be wires, black wires grow on her head.
  5 I have seen roses damask'd red and white,
    But no such roses see I in her cheeks;
    And in some perfumes is there more delight
    Than in the breath that from my mistress reeks.
    I love to hear her speak, yet well I know
 10 That music hath a far more pleasing sound;
    I grant I never saw a goddess go—
    My mistress when she walks treads on the ground,
        And yet, by heaven, I think my love as rare
        As any she belied with false compare.
                        (SHAKESPEARE: *Sonnet 130*)

(d) How still it is; the signal light
    At set of sun shines palely green;
    A thrush sings; other sound there's none,
    Nor traveller to be seen—
                    (DE LA MARE: *The Railway Junction*)

6. Rhythm of Ideas

The rhythmic devices we have looked at so far—syllable-stress,
emphatic stress, phrasing, metre and verse form—have all been
concerned with sound-rhythms of one kind or another. Rhythm can
also be generated structurally. This can be on an obvious level, in the
use of rhyme or refrain (both further kinds of sound-rhythm if you
like), or it can be done more subtly in the repeated turning of the
argument about a central idea, or in the development throughout the
poem of a group of closely associated images. The shape of a poem can
be such that the thoughts repeatedly turn back to the central theme or
situation. Look, for example, at Donne's *A Valediction Forbidding
Mourning*, printed on page 18. Here the mind is in turn directed
along several avenues of proof, each one an attempt to console Donne's
wife in her distress at his parting. The final two lines ring a change
with the implied warning that she should remain faithful to him during
his absence so that he himself will return true. But even this jest,

suggesting, as it does, his anxiety about her loyalty to him, is really another way of 'forbidding' her grief and should reassure her of his lasting affection for her. The slight change in key that these lines give to the rhythm of ideas developed in the poem makes a very satisfying conclusion to the whole.

C Practice

The poems which follow have been selected because any balanced attempt at practical criticism of them is likely to involve discussion of rhythm in one or more of the aspects of it presented in this chapter.

Working either in small discussion groups or individually, consider each one, paying special attention to the features of rhythm in each that seem to you interesting. At the end of the selection are some notes on the first four poems. These notes were made following discussions on the poems with our own pupils. After you have made your own notes, compare them with ours.

(a) I Sing of a Maiden
I sing of a maiden
    That is makeless;
King of all kings
    To her son she ches.

5 He came all so still,
    There his mother was,
As dew in April
    That falleth on the grass.

He came all so still
10   To his mother's bower,
As dew in April
    That falleth on the flower.

He came all so still—
    There his mother lay,
15 As dew in April
    That falleth on the spray.

Mother and maiden
    Was never none but she;
  Well may such a lady
20   God's mother be.

ANON.

(*makeless*—matchless; *ches*—chose)

(*b*) **Slow, Slow, Fresh Fount**

  Slow, slow, fresh fount, keep time with my salt tears;
    Yet slower, yet, O faintly gentle springs:
  List to the heavy part the music bears,
    Woe weeps out her division when she sings.
5   Droop herbs, and flowers;
        Fall grief in showers;
        Our beauties are not ours:
          O, I could still
  (Like melting snow upon some craggy hill,)
10   Drop, drop, drop, drop,
  Since nature's pride is, now, a wither'd daffodil.

(BEN JONSON: Cynthia's Revels)

(*c*) **The Sun Rising**

    Busy old fool, unruly Sun,
    Why dost thou thus,
  Through windows, and through curtains call on us?
  Must to thy motions lovers' seasons run?
5   Saucy pedantic wretch, go chide
    Late schoolboys, and sour prentices,
    Go tell Court-huntsmen, that the King will ride,
    Call country ants to harvest offices;
  Love, all alike, no season knows, nor clime,
10 Nor hours, days, months, which are the rags of time.

    Thy beams, so reverend and strong
    Why shouldst thou think?
  I could eclipse and cloud them with a wink,
  But that I would not lose her sight so long:

53

15 If her eyes have not blinded thine,
   Look, and tomorrow late, tell me,
  Whether both the Indias of spice and mine
  Be where thou left'st them, or lie here with me.
  Ask for those Kings whom thou saw'st yesterday,
20 And thou shalt hear, all here in one bed lay.

   She is all States, and all Princes, I,
    Nothing else is.
  Princes do but play us; compar'd to this,
  All honour's mimic, all wealth alchemy.
25   Thou sun art half as happy as we,
    In that the world's contracted thus;
  Thine age asks ease, and since thy duties be
  To warm the world, that's done in warming us.
  Shine here to us, and thou art everywhere;
30 This bed thy centre is, these walls thy sphere.
         JOHN DONNE

(*d*) **Bat**

  At evening, sitting on this terrace,
  When the sun from the west, beyond Pisa, beyond the
    mountains of Carrara
  Departs, and this world is taken by surprise . . .
  When the tired flower of Florence is in gloom beneath the
    glowing
5 Brown hills surrounding . . .

  When under the arches of the Ponte Vecchio
  A green light enters against the stream, flush from the west,
  Against the current of obscure Arno . . .

  Look up, and you see things flying
10 Between the day and the night;
  Swallows with spools of dark thread sewing the shadows
    together.

A circle swoop, and a quick parabola under the bridge arches
Where light pushes through;
A sudden turning upon itself of a thing in the air.
15 A dip to the water.

And you think:
'The swallows are flying so late!'

Swallows?

Dark air-life looping
20 Yet missing the pure loop . . .
A twitch, a twitter, an elastic shudder in flight
And serrated wings against the sky,
Like a glove, a black glove thrown up at the light,
And falling back.

25 Never swallows!
Bats!
The swallows are gone.

At a wavering instant the swallows give way to bats
By the Ponte Vecchio . . .
30 Changing guard.

Bats, and an uneasy creeping in one's scalp
As the bats swoop overhead!
Flying madly.

Pipistrello!
35 Black piper on an infinitesimal pipe.
Little lumps that fly in air and have voices indefinite,
        wildly vindictive;

Wings like bits of umbrella.

Bats!

Creatures that hang themselves up like an old rag, to sleep;
40 And disgustingly upside down.
Hanging upside down like rows of disgusting old rags
And grinning in their sleep.
Bats!

In China the bat is a symbol of happiness.

45 Not for me!

D. H. LAWRENCE

(e) **Virtue**
Sweet day, so cool, so calm, so bright,
The bridal of the earth and sky:
The dew shall weep thy fall tonight;
    For thou must die.

5 Sweet rose, whose hue angry and brave
Bids the rash gazer wipe his eye:
Thy root is ever in its grave,
    And thou must die.

Sweet spring, full of sweet days and roses,
10 A box where sweets compacted lie;
My music shows ye have your closes,
    And all must die.

Only a sweet and virtuous soul,
Like seasoned timber, never gives;
15 But though the whole world turn to coal,
    Then chiefly lives.

GEORGE HERBERT

(f) Sonnet

The world is too much with us; late and soon,
Getting and spending, we lay waste our powers:
Little we see in Nature that is ours;
We have given our hearts away, a sordid boon!
5 This sea that bares her bosom to the moon;
The winds that will be howling at all hours,
And are up-gather'd now like sleeping flowers;
For this, for everything, we are out of tune;
It moves us not. —Great God! I'd rather be
10 A Pagan suckled in a creed outworn;
So might I, standing on this pleasant lea,
Have glimpses that would make me less forlorn;
Have sight of Proteus rising from the sea;
Or hear old Triton blow his wreathed horn.
WILLIAM WORDSWORTH

(g) God's Grandeur

The world is charged with the grandeur of God.
  It will flame out, like shining from shook foil;
  It gathers to a greatness, like the ooze of oil
Crushed. Why do men then now not reck his rod?
5 Generations have trod, have trod, have trod;
  And all is seared with trade; bleared, smeared with toil;
  And wears man's smudge and shares man's smell: the soil
Is bare now, nor can foot feel, being shod.

  And for all this, nature is never spent;
10   There lives the dearest freshness deep down things;
And though the last lights off the black West went
  Oh, morning, at the brown brink eastward, springs—
Because the Holy Ghost over the bent
  World broods with warm breast and with ah! bright wings.
GERARD MANLEY HOPKINS

57

(h) **How Still the Hawk**

How still the hawk
Hangs innocent above
Its native wood:
Distance, that purifies the act
5 Of all intent, has graced
Intent with beauty.
Beauty must lie
As innocence must harm
Whose end (sited
10 Held) is naked
Like the map it cowers on.
And the doom drops:
Plummet of peace
For him who does not share
15 The nearness and the need,
The shrivelled circle
Of magnetic fear.

CHARLES TOMLINSON

Notes

I Sing of a Maiden

The simple delicacy of the metre. It follows the natural rhythms of language but has a beautifully balanced regularity.

The iambic opening to most lines is fittingly reverent—a hushed, tentative approach. The more positive trochaic feet at the start of lines 3, 17, 19 and 20 are suitably firm, confident. Triumphant ending helped in last line by the weight of three heavy stresses:

God's mother be.

The repetition in the three central verses gives feeling of permanence—a static, eternal event? This quality is tempered by two interesting sets of modification from verse to verse: the poem appears to develop in two directions—*mother was . . . mother's bower . . . Mother lay* moves us inwards, approach to the birth itself, while *grass . . . flower . . . spray* is an opening movement, growth, blossoming, fruition—the expanding significance of Christ's birth? This double movement gives balance, poise, tension to the poem.

Slow, Slow Fresh Fount

The heavy rhythms, slowing the pace of the poem, especially in lines 1, 5, 6 and 10 with stressed monosyllables placed together, offer an almost physical experience of the poet's grief. We feel its weight. The movement of the verse contributes almost as much as the emotive value of words like 'slow', 'woe', 'weeps', 'droop', 'grief', 'drop' and 'wither'd'.

The complex verse form creates a kind of tension: we respond to the poignancy of grief that is contained within the framework of a tightly controlled form. (A minority felt that the carefully worked pattern was merely evidence of the artificiality of the poet's feeling.)

The break in the flow of the last line on 'now' enforces upon us the immediacy of the poet's grief and at the same time heightens the trembling effect, through isolation, of the final phrase 'a wither'd daffodil'.

The Sun Rising

This is dramatic verse. The speech rhythms demonstrate the toughness and flexibility of a basically iambic metre. The opening is angry— a heavy first syllable (a trochaic foot) with short vowel and explosive consonant. But there is a slowing and a smoothing out of the rhythm as the poet's temper improves towards the end of the first stanza. We *hear* him growing less irritable and as he turns towards his mistress in lines 9 and 10 the flow of words is smooth, wistful, more drawn-out (long vowels in 'Hours, days, months').

There is a greater control as the poem proceeds. The mood has changed from waking irritability to a whimsical benignity. Note the confident firmness of 'Nothing else is' where the short line of heavy stresses gives added sense of completeness.

There is a rhetorical splendour in certain lines. The speaker enjoys seeming to patronise the sun. The balance of rhythms helps convey this poise:

'Be where thou left'st them, or lie here with me.'
'All honour's mimic; all wealth alchemy.'
'This bed thy centre is, these walls, thy sphere.'

Bat

This is free verse. The rhythms created by word-weighting and phrasing convey atmosphere and evoke emotional response.

The opening is calm. The phrases are quite short but stresses are well spaced so there is no feeling of urgency. Suits leisurely series of visual impressions. Mood is peaceful, warm and lazy.

'Look up' (line 9) brings a sudden change. There is tension in the short phrase, which is followed by a feeling of relief as the rhythms follow the swooping movements and graceful curves of the swallows' flight (lines 11 and 12).

A change again, but this time the pause before the slow question 'Swallows?' (line 18) is more sinister. With the realisation that the swallows have given way to bats—or is it that they were bats all the time? (opinion divided here)—the verse movement becomes nervous, erratic. Notice the twitching rhythms of lines 21 and 22 and contrast them with lines 11 and 12.

The short, emphatic 'Bats!' (lines 26 and 38), crude and explosively spat out, is good support for the disgust the poet speaks of in lines 40–42 and that he implies with phrases like 'Little lumps' and 'wildly vindictive' in line 36.

More shivering rhythms created by very rapid, short syllables in lines 35 and 36 build up the sense of fear and distaste, and we are ready for the emphatic rejection in the two firm stresses of the last line.

Sounds, Rhymes and Forms
A Sound Effects

1. *Introductory*

Poetry is usually intended to be read aloud, and the pleasure we get from it is enhanced by hearing it well read. This section is designed to point out some of the ways in which poets try to use sound to add to their overall effect.

Are there any poems you've read so far in this book whose sounds you've particularly enjoyed?

Can you think of any other writings—speeches or television advertisements, for example—whose authors are consciously trying to manipulate sounds? Talk about them, and try to see what effect the sounds contribute to the total impact of the writing. A contrast between the effects of the original and a paraphrase may help you here. Look back also at the illustration from *The Eve of St. Agnes* on page 28.

2. *Sound and Sense*

It is very difficult to say whether the effect of a given piece of writing is due to its sound rather than to its meaning, or to some special literary quality. Language, after all, consists of sounds to which meanings are attached, and the two are inseparable in the hearer's mind. Here is an extract from Coleridge's *Kubla Khan* in which the sound can be said to add appreciably to the reader's enjoyment:

> In Xanadu did Kubla Khan
> A stately pleasure-dome decree:
> Where Alph, the sacred river, ran
> Through caverns measureless to man
> 5   Down to a sunless sea.

Savour the richness of the words, with their feeling of luxury. Now consider:

> In Bakerloo did Aly Khan
> A stately Hippodrome decree:
> Where Alf, the bread delivery man,
> Brought crumpets in his horse-drawn van
> 5   Down to the A.B.C.

Is the parody a fair comparison with the original?

Are there any words in either extract that still seem to you to carry any particular effect by virtue of their sound?

Consider now this argument by Sir Max Beerbohm:

> What you take to be beauty or ugliness of sound is indeed nothing but beauty or ugliness of meaning. You are pleased by the sound of such words as *gondola, vestments, chancel, ermine, Manor-house* . . . Prepare for a slight shock. *Scrofula, investments, cancer, vermin, warehouse.* Horrible words, are they not? But . . . if gondola were a disease, and if scrofula were a beautiful boat peculiar to a beautiful city, the effect of each word would be exactly the reverse of what it is.

Do you agree?

Has Beerbohm played quite fair with 'gondola/scrofula'?

Which pair of words do you find the most compelling example? Can you improve on it?

Of course, there are cases in which particular sounds working in a particular context can contribute to the writing.

> The hare limp'd trembling through the frozen grass.

and

> 'Tis dark: quick pattereth the flaw-blown sleet

both carry in their rhythms and consonants a representation of the things they are describing. Or do they?

3. *Some practice*

For the first extract printed here, some preparation will be needed. Each member of the group should prepare a reading of the passage—some perhaps could take an unusual, or elaborate, interpretation. Then compare your readings. See what your readings have in common, and how far the writer has forced this reading on you. What is there in the passage to demand that it be read in a particular fashion?

> To-morrow, and to-morrow, and to-morrow,
> Creeps in this petty pace from day to day,
> To the last syllable of recorded time;
> And all our yesterdays have lighted fools
> 5 The way to dusty death. Out, out, brief candle!

Life's but a walking shadow; a poor player,
That struts and frets his hour upon the stage,
And then is heard no more: it is a tale
Told by an idiot, full of sound and fury,
10 Signifying nothing.

(SHAKESPEARE: *Macbeth*)

You may compare the previous passage to the following: Henry V
has been insulted by the gift of tennis balls from the Dauphin:

And tell the pleasant prince this mock of his
Hath turn'd his balls to gun-stones; and his soul
Shall stand sore charged for the wasteful vengeance
That shall fly with them: for many a thousand widows
5 Shall this his mock mock out of their dear husbands;
Mock mothers from their sons, mock castles down;
And some are yet ungotten and unborn
That shall have cause to curse the Dauphin's scorn.

(SHAKESPEARE: *Henry V*)

What emotion is conveyed by this speech?

Is the emotion the only factor that governs the way the speech
should be delivered? What words govern the tone of voice and the
pace of delivery? Why do the last two lines rhyme?

4. *Rhythm as a Sound Effect*

In the section on Rhythm, the various ways of manipulating stress and
stress pattern for poetic effect were pointed out. We are now going to
look at the rhythms that a poet can use independently of his basic
metric pattern when he wishes above all to use the sounds and swing of
his language to get his tone over to his reader. This is one way, clearly,
in which sound can be seen to have an effect beyond that of meaning:
for it is the cumulative effect of many sounds in a particular context,
where the pace of the words can echo, for example, the pace of
thought, and thus add to our understanding of that thought.

Read this poem:

Hurrahing in Harvest

Summer ends now; now, barbarous in beauty, the stooks arise
    Around; up above, what wind-walks! what lovely behaviour
Of silk-sack clouds! has wilder, wilful-wavier
Meal-drift moulded ever and melted across skies?

5 I walk, I lift up, I lift up heart, eyes,
    Down all that glory in the heavens to glean our Saviour;
    And, eyes, heart, what looks, what lips yet gave you a
Rapturous love's greeting of realer, of rounder replies?

And the azurous hung hills are his world-wielding shoulder
10   Majestic—as a stallion stalwart, very-violet-sweet!—
These things, these things were here and but the beholder
    Wanting; which two when they once meet,
The heart rears wings bold and bolder
    And hurls for him, O half hurls earth for him off under his feet.

                                 (G. M. HOPKINS)

What is this poem about?

What feeling does it have?

Do you think it is well titled?

Let us look at how the feeling of the poem is built up. In the first quatrain, the imagery is immediately striking, as are the words in which it is expressed—'wilful-wavier meal-drift' and 'wind-walks', for example. Why does the poet coin such multiple words?

Where do you think the rhythmic climax of the quatrain comes?

Which word do you find most heavily emphasised? Is it an apt one?

Where do you find the rhythmic climax of the sestet?

Though there may be disagreement as to how exactly the poem should be read and where the rhythmic emphasis should be placed, it should be apparent to you how strongly the rhythm of a poem acts as a sound effect to contribute to the feeling, and hence to the total meaning, of the poem. Now consider these questions on the contribution made by other sound effects.

Why does the poet repeat phrases (e.g. lines 11 and 14)?

Why does he change the order of 'heart, eyes' (line 5) to 'eyes, heart' (line 7)?

Why does he repeat consonants (*alliteration*) such as 'm' (line 4), 'r' (line 8) and 'h' (line 14)?

Did you notice the rhymes? How well do you think the poet manages them?

5. *Imitative Sound Effects*

Now look at this extract from a modern version of *Sir Gawayn and the Green Knight*, a poem of about Chaucer's period. Gawayn, one of King Arthur's knights, is about to cut off the Green Knight's head:

> The green knight now kneels down, now lies on the floor,
> Lowers his head a little, and the white flesh displays.
> His lovely long locks he lays over his crown
> To let his naked neck show to the knight.
> 5 Gawayn grips his great axe and gathers to the swing,
> Puts his left foot forward, on the floor for balance,
> Lets it swing swiftly down, sees it land on the skin
> So the champion's sharp edge sheared the bone,
> And sank through the soft flesh and split it in two,
> 10 Till the blade of brown steel bit into the ground:
> The head from its place pitched to the floor.

This poem is obviously written in a different formal pattern from that of the rhymed verse we accept as 'traditional'. Can you see what it is? We will return to the matter of forms later on; meanwhile let us see how this writer uses this form in this poem.

Can you see any particular rhythmic sound effects that seem to you to work well? What words are heavily emphasised?

Is there anywhere where you find *onomatopoeia* (see Glossary) used to strong effect?

What, other than the shape of the verse, does the alliteration add to the poem?

6. Sound for Fun

So far, we have been looking at sounds used to reinforce meaning or to give emphasis. But some poets have found in sound itself their inspiration, or stimulus, and have written with aural pleasure very much in mind. Read, for example, Edith Sitwell:

> When
> Sir
> Beelzebub called for his syllabub in the hotel in Hell
>   Where Proserpine first fell,
> 5 Blue as the gendarmerie were the waves of the sea,
>   (Rocking and shocking the bar-maid).
> Nobody comes to give him his rum but the
> Rim of the sky hippotamus-glum
> Enhances the chances to bless with a benison
> 10 Alfred Lord Tennyson crossing the bar laid
> With cold vegetation from pale deputations
> Of temperance workers (all signed In Memoriam)
> Hoping with glory to trip up the Laureate's feet,
>   (Moving in classical metres) . . .
> 15 Like Balaclava, the lava came down from the
> Roof, and the sea's blue wooden gendarmerie
> Took them in charge while Beelzebub roared for his rum.
>   . . . None of them come!

What does this mean? Does it matter?

What phrases or words in the poem do you find particularly striking? Why?

Are the rhymes effective? Have you noticed all of them?

.   .   .

When Sir Beelzebub is an extreme example of writing with sound in mind. But there are many other poems in which *euphony*, or beauty of sound, plays a considerable part. This anonymous madrigal was originally set to music:

Philistus' Farewell to False Clorinda

'Clorinda false, adieu; thy love torments me:
Let Thirsis have thy heart, since he contents thee.
      Oh grief and bitter anguish!
        For thee I languish.
5   Fain I, alas, would hide it,
        Oh, but who can abide it?
        I can, aye cannot I abide it?
      Adieu, adieu then;
        Farewell!
10   Leave my death now desiring,
      For thou hast thy requiring.'
      Thus spake Philistus, on his hook re-lying;
        And sweetly fell a-dying.

What is the feeling of this poem? Comment on the effect of the word 'sweetly' (line 13).

Why do you think this might be suitable for singing?

How would you describe the sound of the whole? Are there any harsh sounds?

7. *Some other Sound Effects*

This section cannot be exhaustive: there are too many kinds of sound effect in poetry to catalogue here. There is no need to do this, for as long as you have some comprehension of how sound can work, you do not need the technical names for what the poet is doing. We are now going to look briefly at two other devices, less to know what they are called than to see further the way in which sound contributes to the overall meaning of a poem.

First, read this extract from Wilfred Owen's *Exposure*:

Our brains ache, in the merciless iced east winds that knive us . . .
Wearied we keep awake because the night is silent . . .
Low, drooping flares confuse our memory of the salient . . .
Worried by silence, sentries whisper, curious, nervous,
5   But nothing happens.

67

Watching, we hear the mad gusts tugging on the wire,
Like twitching agonies of men among its brambles.
Northward, incessantly, the flickering gunnery rumbles
Far off, like a dull rumour of some other war.
10   What are we doing here?

What do you notice about the ends of the lines?
Why do you think Owen uses this half-rhyme?
Do you think it is apt in this context?
Discuss the effect of the following:

'merciless iced east winds that knive us' (line 1)
'Worried by silence, sentries whisper, curious, nervous' (line 4)
'mad gusts' (line 6)
'rumbles/Far off' (lines 8–9).

The special effect of half-rhyme can be paralleled by some of the effects of pure rhyme, which can be used to point a thought or a rhetorical trick of expression.

No louder shrieks to pitying heaven are cast
When husbands, or when lap-dogs, breathe their last.

Know then thyself, presume not God to scan:
The proper study of mankind is man.

In the first of these, the anti-climax of the linking of husbands and lap-dogs is pointed by the simple, emphatic rhyme: in the second, the dogmatic statement is given added weight and completeness by the rhyme.

8. *More Practice*

Now try to analyse the part that sound plays in the following extracts:

The river's tent is broken; the last fingers of leaf
Clutch and sink into the wet bank. The wind
Crosses the brown land, unheard.
                    (T. S. ELIOT)

(Why is 'clutch' the first, and 'wind' the last, word in the line?)

. . . How a lush-kept plush-capped sloe
     Will, mouthed to flesh-burst,
Gush!—flush the man, the being with it, sour or sweet,
Brim, in a flash, full!

(G. M. Hopkins)

True Ease in Writing comes from Art, not Chance,
As those move easiest who have learn'd to dance.
'Tis not enough no Harshness gives Offence,
The Sound must seem an Echo to the Sense.
5 Soft is the Strain when Zephyr gently blows,
And the smooth Stream in smoother Numbers flows:
But when loud Surges lash the sounding Shore,
The hoarse, rough Verse shou'd like the Torrent roar.
When Ajax strives, some Rock's vast Weight to throw,
10 The Line too labours, and the Words move slow.

(Alexander Pope)

I am grown peaceful as old age to-night.
I regret little, I would change still less.
Since there my past life lies, why alter it?

(R. Browning)

When the hounds of spring are on winter's traces,
    The mother of months in meadow or plain
Fills the shadows and windy places
    With lisp of leaves and ripple of rain;
5 And the brown bright nightingale amorous
Is half assuaged for Itylus,
For the Thracian ships and the foreign faces,
    The tongueless vigil, and all the pain.

(A. Swinburne)

B Forms

1. Rhyme and Structure

Any mention of rhyme brings us to the consideration of the part it plays in giving poetry a shape that emphasises its unity. Poetry is a controlled way of using language, and one way of showing control is to use a pattern of sound as well as the basic patterns of thought. Here is a simple example, a ballad:

Edward, Edward

1 'Why does your brand sae drap wi' blude,   *blade*
     Edward, Edward?
Why does your brand sae drap wi' blude,
    And why sae sad gang ye, O?'—   *go*
'O I hae kill'd my hawk sae gude,
     Mither, mither;
O I hae kill'd my hawk sae gude,
    And I had nae mair but he, O.'   *no more*

2 'Your hawk's blude was never sae red,
     Edward, Edward;
Your hawk's blude was never sae red,
    My dear son, now tell me, O.' —
'O I hae kill'd my red-roan steed,
     Mither, mither;
O I hae kill'd my red-roan steed,
    That erst was sae fair and free, O.'   *formerly*

3 'Your steed was auld, and ye hae got mair,   *old*
     Edward, Edward;
Your steed was auld, and ye hae got mair;
    Some other dule ye dree, O!' —   *grief you suffer*
'O I hae kill'd my father dear,
     Mither, mither;
O I hae kill'd my father dear,
    Alas and wae is me, O!'

4 'And whatten penance will ye dree for that,
        Edward, Edward?
  And whatten penance will ye dree for that?
      My dear son, now tell me, O.'—
  'I'll set my feet in yonder boat,
        Mither, mither;
  I'll set my feet in yonder boat,
      And I'll fare over the sea, O.'

5 'And what will ye do wi' your tow'rs and your ha',   *hall*
        Edward, Edward?
  And what will ye do wi' your tow'rs and your ha',
      That were sae fair to see, O?'—
  'I'll let them stand till they down fa',
        Mither, mither;
  I'll let them stand till they down fa',
      For here never mair maun I be, O.'   *must*

6 'And what will ye leave to your bairns and your wife,   *children*
        Edward, Edward?
  And what will ye leave to your bairns and your wife,
      When ye gang owre the sea, O?'—
  'The warld's room: let them beg through life,
        Mither, mither;
  The warld's room: let them beg through life;
      For them never mair will I see, O.'

7 'And what will ye leave to your ain mother dear,   *own*
        Edward, Edward?
  And what will ye leave to your ain mither dear,
      My dear son, now tell me, O?'—
  'The curse of hell from me sall ye bear,   *shall*
        Mither, mither;
  The curse of hell from me sall ye bear:
      Sic counsels ye gave to me, O!'   *such*

                                        (ANON.)

The structure of this ballad is obvious enough. Why is the repetition
well suited to this particular poem?

Does the rhyme help to shape the poem as much as the repetition of phrases?

Do you find this poem at all loosely written?

2. *The Sonnet*

Now for a form complete in itself. Although you've read the whole of *Edward, Edward* and can see the cumulative effect of the repeated structure, the formal unit is only 8 lines long. The sonnet, however, is a form that stands on its own—it makes a complete poem, without repetition of the structural unit. Read this one:

> Loving in truth, and fain in verse my love to show
> That the dear She might take some pleasure of my pain—
> Pleasure might cause her read, reading might make her know,
> Knowledge might pity win, and pity grace obtain—
> 5   I sought fit words to paint the blackest face of woe,
> Studying inventions fine, her wits to entertain:
> Oft turning others' leaves, to see if thence would flow
> Some fresh and fruitful showers upon my sun-burn'd brain.
>   But words came halting forth, wanting Invention's stay—
> 10 Invention, Nature's child, fled stepdame Study's blows—
> And others' feet still seemed but strangers in my way.
> Thus great with child to speak, and helpless in my throes,
>   Biting my truant pen, beating myself for spite,
>   'Fool,' said my Muse to me, 'look in thy heart and write.'
>
>   (SIR PHILIP SIDNEY)

What is the rhyme-scheme?

How do the poet's sentences and thoughts fit into this rhyme scheme?

Does the layout of the poem on the printed page reflect the patterns of thought and rhyme?

Is there any significance in the closeness of the sounds 'flow'/'blows' and 'brain'/'way'?

A possible appreciation of the effect of the form in the Sidney sonnet might read:

This sonnet opens, as is the convention, with an octet divided into two quatrains. Each quatrain is concerned with a separate thought—the first with the capturing of the interest of 'the dear She', with its careful rhetorical balancing of phrases, and the second with the seeking of 'fit words'. But there is only one sentence, and the structure reflects this in maintaining the same rhymes through the octet.

It is followed by a sestet. The rhymes are those of a quatrain and a couplet, but the thought divides with the sentence ending at the end of line 11. Sidney has chosen a different rhyme for the third quatrain, but it is only slightly different; this serves to emphasise the unity of the sonnet. Finally, the couplet, with its simple and complete rhyme, serves to drive home the final line, giving a sense of completion and finality to the poem.

Do you agree?

Now read this sonnet by Milton:

On His Blindness

When I consider how my light is spent,
   Ere half my days in this dark world and wide,
   And that one Talent which is death to hide
   Lodg'd with me useless, though my soul more bent
5 To serve therewith my Maker, and present
   My true account, lest he returning chide;
   'Doth God exact day-labour, light deny'd?'
   I fondly ask: but Patience, to prevent
That murmur, soon replies, 'God doth not need
10   Either man's work or His own gifts. Who best
   Bear His mild yoke, they serve Him best: His state
Is Kingly. Thousands at His bidding speed
   And post o'er land and ocean without rest:
   They also serve who only stand and wait.'

What is the rhyme-scheme of this sonnet? In what ways does it differ from that of the previous example?

What effect on the poem do you think the tendency of the rhymes to fall into couplets in the octet has had?

Notice the free running-on of the sentences from line to line. How do you account for this?

Analyse the effect of this sestet.

C Conclusion

In this brief look at two of the forms that have been used by English poets, you ought to have discovered that it is not the form itself that matters, so much as its handling in particular instances. What is more important in the treatment of structure is to take each example on its merits: the structure used by, say, Shakespeare will not redeem shoddy or inaccurate or unpoetic writing by an imitator. In this, structure is like all literary techniques—they are only the tools used by a poet to achieve his work of communication. This equally applies to the sound effects dealt with earlier in this chapter. No one sound carries, of its nature, an effect or meaning or feeling that a poet can rely on to communicate for him with his reader. To use sounds, he must place them into a context where they are seen to work with his rhythm, his vocabulary, his imagery and everything else that is part of the meaning of his poem.

3 THREE POEMS AND THEIR CRITICS

There are three poems in this chapter, each followed by a series of critical comments. The material needs private study first of all and can then be discussed.

By this stage, readers of this book will be familiar with critical terms and methods; some may feel that in criticising poetry there is always a 'right answer' if only they could see it, while others may be so convinced that there can never be anything of the sort that they are inclined to dismiss most of what has been said so far as academic irrelevance. Neither attitude is really fair—there is never one absolutely right answer which will render all the others wrong; but there *are* ways of arriving at an answer which are likely to be more fruitful than others.

A 'Appointment'

This section demonstrates a number of ways (both fruitful and unfruitful) of criticising a poem. All the critics involved were comparatively inexperienced and all were writing fast at short notice; they fell into many of the traps that wait for any critic who is not thinking carefully, but they also produced some valuable ideas. The commentary tries to show how they went wrong and how they went right.

> **Appointment**
> Of the five times of day, the one I fear the most
> Is not the knocking dawn, or the morning false
> With promise, nor the soft elusive afternoon
> Nor night of silver-mooned security,
> 5 But evening-time, sad with memory
> And fear around the turning of a lane;
> A great dumb rocking horse that waits for me
> Beyond the long slow fade of afterday.
> This silent evening holds more pain than night.

10 Dead are the dead, but dying seems so long:
   Not yet, I say, and clutch the tepid light
   For me the weaving darkness shall not come.

                              COLIN ROWBOTHAM

The author of this poem was a sixth former when he wrote it. We asked a number of boys (of varying ages and studying different subjects) to read it and write down their immediate reactions.

Some writers were prevented from appreciating this, or any other, poem by certain basic faults in their method of approach. Consider these comments:

  (i)   I don't like this poem because I haven't got a sense of poetry.
  (ii) I cannot agree with 'soft elusive afternoon' which somehow conjures up a picture of snow falling on a mountainside, the idea of which doesn't fit into the poem at all.
  (iii) The five times of day represent the five stages of life, and each stage is accurately described; for example, 'silver-mooned security' refers to middle age when one has married, and has a steady job with two or three children nearly grown up.
  (iv) Why should the author trouble us with his problems?

Each of these points will be mentioned later, but it is worth your pausing here to discuss them carefully—*what are the faults which they exemplify?*

Those critics who were prepared to read the poem as they would any other written communication responded much more freely to it:

  (v)   This poem agrees with my thoughts. The evening, with its half-light, is very strange. Almost frightening. It has a deep meaning. It describes the evening very well. The 'great dumb rocking horse' is all the things which could be round the corner. A fierce dog, a strange man, or a large bat. If he was alone, no one within miles, it might be a vampire, a werewolf, or a ghost. The writer must have experienced an evening like this. It is excellent. It has an eerie atmosphere. Quiet, the grey of dusk, and all the other things which make this poem so real. The writer has transformed these things into words, and a poem.

This writer has sensed the 'mood' of the poem and related it to his own feelings. Several other writers liked the poem because they had felt about evening in the same way as the poet. *Can poetry only communicate on such a basis of shared experience?*

One so often hears a poem dismissed as being about things outside the reader's range of experience; yet sometimes shared experience can be a positive hindrance to understanding. The rocking horse in *Appointment*, for instance, caused many people trouble.

(vi) When he refers to the rocking horse, he is going back to boyhood when that faithful fluffy rocking horse always waited to take him to the land where he could have £5 pocket money, drive a Jag and shoot all the Indians.

This critic has failed to perceive the general mood of the poem, and has been led astray by memories of childhood which are his own and not the poet's. It is clear that whatever the rocking horse represents it is *not* pleasant or happy; many people may think of their rocking horses with affection, but this poet associates his with 'evening time, *sad* with memory and *fear*'. The next critic is more lucky, because he happens to think of rocking horses as sad, but he hasn't understood the poem any better; his horse still has nothing to do with fear.

(vii) Rocking horses are sad creatures; they never smile and are subjected to every conceivable insult over the years. One always imagines a rocking horse crying—I do.

This third writer has recognised that the poet's ideas about the horse and the evening may not be the same as his own.

(viii) He differs from many people in not thinking, as I do, of the evening as being a calm, peaceful time but more as a time when he feels unprotected. I think the rocking horse is meant to be a symbol of his fear of something round the corner, big and moving and evil for him.

There was an astonishing range of interpretations put on the rocking horse—one critic saw it as a coffin and another as a bus!—but they fell into two main groups: some critics, like the two above, saw the horse as an image of happy childhood memories; most of the rest thought it was in some way connected with death.

(ix) It means he is turning a corner in his life and is in some way confronted with death itself. A simplified explanation would be that of a man turning a blind corner and suddenly seeing the hooves of a horse trampling him into the ground.

(x) The great dumb rocking horse is his fear which can't be budged from his mind but just moves on the same spot sometimes rocking to the back of his mind and sometimes to the front but there all the time . . . or . . . it is death which is so near but keeps rocking away and then comes near again. It waits for him behind the afterday—the evening in which he is dying—but can't get near enough to him.

Some writers also attempted to explain the origin of the image:

(xi) The poet is remembering perhaps a rocking horse he had in childhood. For some reason he is afraid of coming across it suddenly (perhaps when he was a child one night a car's head-lights flashed across the horse's face and this startled him . . . Ever since he has been subconsciously afraid of suddenly being faced with this frightening image . . .).

What do you understand by the rocking horse? Has it got anything to do with death?

A satisfactory interpretation of this image can only be found (if at all) when the poem's subject is understood. As somebody said, 'Appointment with what?' Before discussing this question, consider these two comments:

(xii) One can solve it like a mathematical problem.
(xiii) 'Appointment with Death' would be a fuller title but this would give away the subject of the poem immediately, if poetry is meant to make one think.

Is there any foundation for this belief that poetry is a kind of guessing game in which the poet conceals his answers? Or does 'thinking' about poetry require something more than ingenuity?

Why does the title not say what, or whom, the appointment is with?

Here are two more comments about the title:

(xiv) The title tells us that the poem is about the meeting of two entities—life and death.
(xv) The title itself suggests an unwelcome appointment with somebody—or something—rather as if he were walking the plank.

Few critics were content to say that *Appointment* was about 'the five times of day'. Many decided it was about the 'five stages of human life'—birth, youth, middle age, old age and death. One who held this opinion said:

(xvi) This idea is easily grasped and therefore good in this respect.

This critic was a scientist; it would be interesting to know whether he finds relativity easy to grasp or whether he dismisses it as 'a bad idea in this respect'. It would also be interesting to hear him argue with writer (xiii), since their views about clarity of subject-matter seem directly opposed.

How far should a poet be expected to restrict himself to ideas which are 'easily grasped'? Can we draw a distinction between difficulty and obscurity in a poem? Can either be justified?

It is not perhaps quite so easy to see this poem as being entirely about life and death. Only the tenth line actually refers to dying—can it be merely a metaphor? To explain 'knocking dawn' as a reference to the child kicking its way out of the mother, or 'weaving darkness' as something to do with shrouds is ingenious but not altogether convincing.

What do you think the poem means?

(xvii) It seems to be either an actual day compared metaphorically with death, or death compared metaphorically with the end of a day.

Some critics who felt this ambiguity were irritated by it. 'I cannot make it mean what I want it to mean', complained one, giving up after a long struggle. Small wonder he was irritated—imagine trying to make any piece of writing (a motor car handbook, for instance) mean what you want it to mean instead of trying to find out what it has to tell you! However, the ambiguity of *Appointment* is certainly difficult.

Is this ambiguity intended by the poet? If so, did he intend us to choose between one meaning and another, or to entertain two (or more) in our minds at once?

Now let us consider more fully the mood of the poem and the effect of its imagery and language. First, here is a selection of immediate responses from some very young critics:

(xviii) pretty disgusting . . . stupid . . . rather boring . . . hard to understand . . . sentimental . . . mysterious . . . rather weird, reminding me of 'The Hound of the Baskervilles' . . . a very moving poem; it seems as if he is in a dream . . . frightening . . . spooky!

Again there are negative reactions, probably caused by the difficulty of the poem's subject; but there are also positive *emotional* reactions even when the subject is not understood.

What in the poem, apart from the subject, could have produced these reactions?

Words and patterns of words are the poet's tools. An awareness of vocabulary is an essential part of accurate reading. Some people, for instance, read the last line of *Appointment* as a flat statement and so found it silly—of course the darkness must come for the poet as for everybody else. The punctuation is certainly no help, but the words carry their own meaning:

(xix) . . . the poem is meant to be desperate at the end, especially in the last line but one. The word 'clutch' conveys a feeling of desperate speed, and does not convey the feeling of a hand slowly closing.

The same writer went on to point out that this speed only occurs at the end, and singled out 'long', 'great', 'slow', 'fade', and 'wait' as drawn-out words used 'seemingly to signify the passing of time'.

Here are two more comments on the poem's vocabulary:

(xx) Personally, I think evening *is* the gloomiest part of the day—for isn't everything dark and dreary, and yet light as well? There is no sun and no moon—just, as the poet says, 'tepid' light.

(xxi) 'The soft elusive afternoon'—the consonants suggest the pleasant warmth of this short period. The sibilants in the next line just recall that slight coldness of moonlight. 'Beyond the long slow fade of afterday'—this is a beautiful line with long, slow vowels.

Meaning and sound are very close here. *How much more can be said about the poem's vocabulary and sound-patterns?* Did sound-effects of this kind play some part in evoking such comments as 'spooky', 'mysterious' and so on from the younger boys?

We have already seen a number of responses to the imagery of the poem. It is easy to be clever in interpreting images. One critic saw a highly improbable link between 'silver' and 'security': the poet could hardly have intended 'silver' to be taken financially, or else he would have found even more security in the golden sun of day. On the other hand, the same writer suggested a connection between the movement of the rocking horse, the process of weaving, and the cycle of the times of day. Such a connection may well not have been consciously intended by the poet; but his mind is working with images of relentless, cyclic change and so the suggestion is by no means absurd.

What else may be said about the imagery of this poem?

There are several other aspects of the poem which are worth discussing. One writer commented:

(xxii) I like the way the poet rules out all the other times of day until there is only one left, the one he hates.

Some people complained that the last line was too abrupt an ending —the poet had run out of things to say. Several young critics resented the lack of rhyme; slightly older ones, more attentively, noticed that there is in fact a little rhyme and objected to its accidental character; the sixth formers ignored the matter altogether. And everybody ignored metre and rhythm—*why?* (Before you decide there isn't any, look back at the comments of writer (xix).)

In this section, as elsewhere, the value of a full, imaginative response to a poem has been stressed. The word 'full' may sound a cliché in this context, but its meaning is important and can be illustrated. Some of our critics, like writer (ii), considered the poem entirely from their own experience; they responded imaginatively but not fully—a poem is a meeting-point between reader and writer, and the reader is no more entitled to read without thought for the writer than the writer is entitled to write without thought for the reader. Some critics, like writer (i), were prevented from enjoying the poem by an automatic defence mechanism which came into action as soon as the words on the page were recognised as 'poetry'. Some, like writer (iii), simply couldn't read; and some, like (xii), were too anxious to work out a watertight meaning. Writer (iv) was not prepared to respond at all— this is not just a reluctance to make the effort needed to understand poetry; it is a failure to be interested in other human beings.

The best writers at all levels were those who approached the poem with open minds, ready to work on, and be worked on by, what the poet had to say; and who then made the effort to analyse their reactions.

This section has been based on a schoolboy's poem and the immediate reactions to it of other schoolboys. We end with one such reaction in its entirety, and some informal comments on the poem by the poet himself (these comments are taken from a recorded discussion which took place before this section was even planned). Neither of these two appendices is intended to provide final answers, but they may help to round off discussion. You may find it useful to write a considered criticism of the poem for yourself to organise the conclusions you have come to.

(xxiii) The basic imagery of this poem is an old one—day for life and night for death—evening the long, slow time of dying. But it is not death that the poet fears but the dying:

> This silent evening holds more pain than night.
> Dead are the dead, but dying seems so long:

It is difficult to say whether the pain of day's slow death in the evening is itself a subject, separate from the long dying of man for which it stands as a metaphor. Perhaps the poet, as so many do, makes his metaphor a subject in itself giving the poem two, intertwined so as to be almost one.

There is 'fear around the turning of a lane' but dark-alley-fear is the night's product and does not belong to twilight and the evening. Perhaps 'the turning of a lane' is imagery for the blind step into the night, the final plunge which is the end of dying and the beginning of death.

After the turning there is something waiting for him in, or beyond, the darkness—'a great dumb rocking horse'. Is this, in Freudian psychology, a repressed symbol or memory of a dark attic of his childhood, the horse standing alone, proud in the darkness, overwhelming in its potential power? Thus it would become a symbol of the terrible unknown—or rather the terrible half-known of the darkness, the two intermingled darknesses of night and death.

There is a last desperate, and vain, snatch at life: almost a prayer:

> For me the weaving darkness shall not come.

82

The poet uses unusual adjectives to good effect: the 'knocking dawn' to rouse him, the morning 'false with promise'—holding possibilities of success and achievement, many of which will not bear fruit. The evening in its dying is 'sad', and later on 'silent'—dying is long and slow and silent.

'The weaving darkness' is weaving—evil like a serpent.

(xxiv) The poem was pretty much inspired by actual events . . . its main inspiration comes from long, unpleasant journeys on the motorways. This is why I treat the evening as a Limbo time between home and destination, or life and death. Waiting for someone to die is much worse than the actual death when it comes; this is the point of 'Dead are the dead, but dying seems so long.'

The 'great dumb rocking horse' refers to a recurrent childhood fear I had of seeing a huge silent rocking horse suddenly appear around the corner of a country lane. This is how it ties in with the motorways . . . The thing is that it is rather a horrific image, crudely painted with huge staring eyes . . .

In the beginning of the poem, about the five times of day, I wanted to contrast the essential associations of the various times. For instance, the morning is uncomfortable: it knocks inside your head and wakes you up. The rest of the poem is an attempt to compare evening with the process of dying. Even though you see others die you really know that you yourself aren't going to die.

B 'A slumber did my spirit seal'

This section consists of a very short poem by Wordsworth and comments on it by three experienced critics. They find a great many ideas in the poem: indeed, it may be felt that some of these ideas are not really there at all. This is clearly a central topic for discussion; but first, as always, the poem needs to be read with careful attention.

(i) This is the last poem of a sequence known as the Lucy Poems, written by Wordsworth in 1799 . . . It is a tiny poem, with complete simplicity of diction: only one word, Latin and cosmic, comes into it with a kind of resonance. Listen:

> A slumber did my spirit seal;
>   I had no human fears:
> She seemed a thing that could not feel
>   The touch of earthly years.

> 5 No motion has she now, no force;
>   She neither hears nor sees,
> Rolled round in earth's diurnal course,
>   With rocks, and stones, and trees.

The strange thing about this poem is that it seems to include something unspoken: that lies, as it were, *between* the two verses. Consider the first. It is highly complex, with a suggestion of a trance effect;

> A slumber did my spirit seal

as in the past he had been isolated, numbed in his consciousness. The word *seal* is strange; suggesting, perhaps, secrecy, isolation. Notice how the vowels are modulated, how the sibilant s's seem to quicken the line till the clenching of it on the final word.

84

In the next line—

I had no human fears

and the fourth word seems to carry a slightly heavier stress:
human contrasted with *spirit*.

She seemed a thing—

—a *thing*, almost inanimate, as if the poet is watching her from
a distance; it is as if she possessed a statuesque quality, to be
preserved and cherished, inviolable by time. Against this the
word *touch* comes almost with a shock: though it is a complex
word, suggesting both tenderness, lightness, and (in the context)
something inexorable too. And the touch of *earthly* years closes
up the word-ranks of the stanza: *earthly*, *human*, *spirit*.

She dies, and there is a pause while the full implications of the
event grows in the poet's mind. We have moved from the past
into the present. There is no *seeming*; the girl is dead. The world
of nature remains, and she is identified with it. Between the two
stanzas there is, unspoken, the poet's knowledge of his loss. The
first verse was secure, almost arrogant in security. In the interval
he has had to reconsider all his values, all that his *sealed* spirit had
turned away. And the emotion in the last stanza seems to me
capable of interpretation in two ways. (Great poetry often does
just this thing: perhaps giving back, like a mirror, the mood of
the reader.) From one point of view it is a cry of pain; pain under
great control; reticent in its understatement, for it is thus that
great literature conveys in simplicity its moments of the utmost
tension. In another mood I find in it an acceptance, a humility as
contrasted with the earlier arrogance. The world of nature
remains, and she is absorbed into it. In order that this absorption,
this fusion, may be stated more fully, the cosmic motion of the
globe is emphasised:

Rolled round in earth's diurnal course

Diurnal—the heavy latinised word, carrying the main stress of the
line, suggests the remorseless unending motion of the universe.
(Many poets have used, for some such purpose as this, the Latin-
rooted words that lie deep in our consciousness. Remember that,

till recently, Latin was the speech of all science, philosophy, theology. It brings out of the past an accumulated seriousness that no other language can give.)

She dies, and is *rolled round*, in peace or in helpless passivity, as you will, with rocks and stones and trees. Perhaps this is subjective, but I find in these three words a progressive lightening, as it were, of the tension. The rock is to me the menacing, the oppressive thing; stones are smaller, less hostile, but still, in the language of imagery, dead and cold; trees, by contrast, suggest deep-rooted solidity, and yet a life unified with earth and sky. Perhaps it is for this reason that I feel this sense of resignation, of acceptance, of the exchange of one kind of life for a different kind, of absorption into the body of the universe.

T. R. HENN[1]

(ii) The resonance of [this] little poem is achieved by a high pressure of emotion, by a simplicity of language which tautens this emotion, and by a simple contrast of related viewpoints. In the first stanza, Wordsworth is saying that, when Lucy was alive, he could not associate her with mortality. In the second, the position is reversed: it is Lucy now who is sealed in slumber: she, who 'seemed a thing that could not feel/The touch of earthly years', is, now at their mercy—'rolled round in earth's diurnal course', passive, insentient, like the rocks and stones and trees. The switch from subjective to objective, and from life to death, is the more powerful for being made without warning, undemonstratively.

C. DAY LEWIS[2]

(iii) The ironies that have been pursued in poetry for the last several decades are not plentiful in Wordsworth, but they pervade this poem from its first line, 'A slumber did my spirit seal'. Misinterpreting her vitality, the speaker slept, until her permanent sleep awakened him. 'She seemed a thing that could not feel The touch of earthly years'; but in fact she could feel then what

[1] *The Apple and the Spectroscope*, Methuen, 1951.
[2] *The Lyric Impulse*, Chatto and Windus, 1965.

she cannot now. When his spirit slept, she 'seemed a thing'; now, with rocks and trees, she is a thing. It seemed she could not grow old; in fact she did not. She seemed ageless; her energy, which according to Newtonian physics is never to be lost, measures eternity in its diurnal round. Her force and motion continue—no longer hers. As often in elegy, the theme involves the vanity of human consciousness. The endless course includes minor rocks and major stones, in the cycle from people and trees to dust to stone to rocks to dust to organic life and around again.

CARL WOODRING[1]

C 'To Autumn'

Keats's ode *To Autumn*, which is the subject of the passages which follow, is printed on page 22. Read it again carefully before going any further.

This section consists of Keats's only comments on the poem, and three pieces of criticism. It will be seen that the critics differ strongly in their opinions. Is it possible to say that some of them are wrong? Has Professor Herford, for instance, really read the poem carefully? Is Arnold Davenport justified in going far beyond the remarks in Keats's own letter? How successful is Professor Knight in describing more than one level of meaning in the poem?

(i) How beautiful the season is now—How fine the air. A temperate sharpness about it. Really, without joking, chaste weather—Dian skies—I never lik'd stubble-fields so much as now—Aye better than the chilly green of Spring. Somehow a stubble-plain looks warm—in the same way that some pictures look warm—This struck me so much in my Sunday's walk that I composed upon it.

JOHN KEATS[2]

Wordsworth, Houghton Mifflin, Boston, 1965.
Writing to J. H. Reynolds from Winchester, Tuesday 21 September 1819.

(ii) In *To Autumn*, finally, written after an interval of some months [after the other odes], the sense that beauty, though not without some glorious compensation, perishes, which, in varying degrees, dominates these three odes, yields to a serene and joyous contemplation of beauty itself. The 'season of mellow fruitfulness' wakens no romantic vision, no romantic longing, like the nightingale's song; it satisfies all senses, but enthralls and intoxicates none; everything breathes contented fulfilment without satiety, and beauty, too, is fulfilled and complete. Shelley, whose yet greater ode was written a few weeks later, gloried in the 'breath of autumn's being'—the wild west wind as the forerunner and 'creator' of spring. Keats feels here no need either of prophecy or of retrospect. If, for a moment, he asks 'Where are the songs of spring?' it is only to reply 'Think not of them, thou hast thy music too'. This is the secret of his strength, if, also, of his limitation—to be able to take the beauty of the present moment so completely into his heart that it seems an eternal possession.   C. H. HERFORD[1]

(iii) Critical comment on *To Autumn* has generally agreed that it is the most mature and satisfying of the Odes; and it is pretty generally agreed that it is the most objective and impersonal of them. It is commonly regarded as an evocation of the sounds and sights of autumn, expressive of placid fulfilment and having no further suggestions. C. H. Herford's paragraph on the poem in the *Cambridge History* represents the general view . . . This reading is obviously possible or it would not be so widely accepted; and it is apparently supported by Keats's own reference to the poem in his letter . . . Yet there are details in the poem that suggest something that is hardly compatible with a simple mood of satisfied fulfilment. 'Where are the songs of Spring? Ay, where are they?'—that has an indisputable note in it of the sad longing for what was lovely and is gone; the 'wailful choir' of gnats that 'mourn', the light wind that 'lives and dies,' the day which, though bloomed, is 'soft-dying,' the sleeper 'drows'd with the fume of poppies'—these are touches which come closer to the world of the *Ode to a Nightingale* than to happy fulfilment, and

---

[1] *The Cambridge History of English Literature*, Vol. XII, Cambridge University Press, 1915.

suggest that there is more in the poem than the naïve celebration of fruitfulness . . . It is in fact my purpose to suggest that readings of the Herford kind are seriously wrong and do not do justice to the poem. As I read it,

> Where are the songs of Spring? Ay, where are they?
> Think not of them, thou has thy music too

is not a momentary intrusion but the point of the whole poem.

The central element in the concept of autumn created by the poem is that the season is a boundary, a space between two opposite conditions, a moment of poise when one movement culminates and the succeeding movement has scarcely begun. Keats begins deftly touching in these opposites from the first line: 'mists' and 'mellow fruitfulness'; 'bosom-friend, conspiring'; 'load, bless'; and the desirable apples nevertheless 'bend' the old ('mossed') trees that bear them. Then follow three lines that appear to me univalent evocations of simple ripeness and fruitfulness, but the ambivalent note recurs in 'set budding, later flowers', collocating beginnings and endings; and there is a suggestion of fulness and of loss together in 'until they think warm days will never cease . . . o'er-brimmed', while 'warm days, summer, clammy cells' echo the initial contrasts of mists and mellowness.

The two ideas of pause and of opposites continue in the next stanza. The hook 'spares the next swath' for a moment. Since one does not *spare* anybody something pleasant but only something painful, it is inevitably suggested that while from one point of view the reaping of the grain may be a good, from another it is not—in fact it involves the destruction of the 'twin'd flowers'. The furrow is 'half-reap'd', the brook is a boundary over which a figure is seen in the poised act of stepping . . .

The music of autumn which ends the poem is a music of living and dying, of staying and departure, of summer-winter. The wailful choir of small gnats rises and falls as the gusts of the light wind live or die—a beautiful symbol of the generations that fall and rise and in autumn yield place, the old to the young. (In the context of the ideas that I suggest the poem contains, the reading 'sallows'—willows, with their connotations of sorrow, loss and bereavement—seems a more appropriate word than the 'shallows' which is printed by Garrod in his edition.) The 'full-grown lambs' is a phrase that has been objected to on the common sense grounds that a full-grown lamb is not a lamb any longer, but is either a ewe or a ram. But it is a phrase that is fully justified on this reading of the poem: that which was a lamb in the spring is now full-grown and on the point of superseding the generation of its begetters . . . The red-breast that whistles from the garden-croft is characteristically a winter bird and remains in England; the swallow is proverbially the bird of summer and leaves the country when summer is over: its departure is the signal for the beginning of winter . . .

I would argue, then, that Herford was wrong in saying that *To Autumn*, unlike the *Nightingale* and the *Grecian Urn*, does not include the 'sense that beauty, though not without some glorious compensation, perishes'. On the contrary, central to the poem is the sense that a new good is purchased only at the price of the loss of a former good. Far from being an objective, self-sufficient evocation of the 'beauty of the present moment' it is, as Mr. J. M. Murry once suggested, a projection in image and symbol of the calm Shakespearian vision: 'Man must abide his going hence, even as his coming hither. Ripeness is all' . . . [1]

ARNOLD DAVENPORT[2]

(iv) There is a fertility and ripeness in his poetry, whether in his nature impressionism or imaginative probings into human destiny, which gives his ode *To Autumn* something of an inevitable place among his crowning works. It is notable for subtle, and new, consonant-use. The clustering *s*-sounds increase the sense of an almost drowsy fertility reaching its climax in

Thou watchest the last oozings hours by hours.

There is the usual vowel play, especially where slumberous feeling is induced: 'drows'd with the fume of poppies'. But there is an opposite, countering, employ of short syllables, especially in the last stanza: 'wailful choir', 'light wind', 'hilly', 'twitter'. The ode moves from a certain sticky interplay of sibilants and rich vowels to a queer thin music where one can delicately feel a

[1] *King Lear*, V, ii, 9.
[2] 'A Note on "To Autumn" ', in *John Keats—a Reassessment*, ed. Kenneth Muir, Liverpool University Press, 1958.

suggestion of fertility and ripeness on the edge of dissolution. Keats's general tendency from the sensuous to the sleepy and spiritual with no conflict is therefore repeated. The first stanza is heavily weighted with natural richness. The second begins to drowse with a remarkable human embodiment of autumn and a fine 'tiptoe' effect in his 'lifted' hair and hook sparing 'the next swath', wherein we can, if we like, feel a tragic pathos further continued in the remorseless god-like figure squeezing every drop of fertility from his own creation. You may, that is, feel a human reference, with suffering as a creative process. Reference of the seasons to human life is the subject of one of Keats's best sonnets, and elsewhere he considers a man who cannot face mortal destiny with acceptance as a 'ripe plum' spoiling its own bloom. Thought of death is unobtrusively present in the bare stubble and sunset of the last stanza. But the 'soft-dying day' has its own beauty. The gnats may 'mourn' in 'wailful choir', but they contribute to a music sweet as spring's. The issue is uncertain as the wind that 'lives or dies' by turns. Now the last four lines begin to swell with new promise in 'full-grown lambs' bleating loud, crickets singing, the robin whistling; and when the music thins again in the masterly reserve of the final line, we may feel in the swallows preparing for their departure a distant, yet distinct, reference to tragic destiny. For, if the new lambs suggest a seasonal continuance within the natural order, as symbols of rebirth, the swallows 'in the skies' may hint some other mysterious migration (the very word 'twitter' has been applied to spirits) within the dimension of eternity, though Keats here attempts no precise definition. The ode is notable for its ability to suggest to the deeps of a sensitive contemplation far more than it says. The word 'soft', always a favourite, occurs three times. The poem is itself soft-voiced: in place of Keats's usual 'full-throated ease' it offers a breathless placidity.

G. WILSON KNIGHT[1]

[1] The Starlit Dome, Methuen 1941.

4 POETRY IN PREPARATION

Each section in this chapter consists of transcripts of some of the various manuscript drafts through which three well-known poems passed before reaching their final form. A close study of these drafts should give some insight into the workings of poets' minds.

The questions which are included are designed to draw attention to the main points of interest. They may be ignored in favour of more informal discussion.

The three poems are important enough to be studied on their own, without reference to the drafts, if so desired.

A Blake's 'Tyger'

1. First Draft

The Tyger

1   1 Tyger Tyger burning bright
    In the forests of the night
    What immortal hand or eye
   ~~Dare~~ ~~Could~~ frame thy fearful symmetry

     ~~Burnt in~~
5   2 ~~In what~~ distant deeps or skies
~~The cruel~~ ~~Burnt the~~ fire of thine eyes
    On what wings dare he aspire
    What the hand dare sieze the fire

    3 And what shoulder & what art
10   Could twist the sinews of thy heart
    And when thy heart began to beat
    What dread hand & what dread feet

    ~~Could fetch it from the furnace deep~~
    ~~And in thy horrid ribs dare steep~~
15   ~~In the well of sanguine woe~~
    ~~In what clay & in what mould~~
    ~~Were thy eyes of fury rolld~~
    Where   where
    4 ~~What~~ the hammer ~~what~~ the chain
    In what furnace was thy brain
                  dread grasp
20   What the anvil what ~~arm~~ ~~arm~~ ~~grasp~~ ~~clasp~~
Dare ~~Could~~ its deadly terrors ~~clasp~~ ~~grasp~~ clasp

    6 Tyger tyger burning bright
    In the forests of the night
    What immortal hand & eye
        frame
25   Dare ~~form~~ thy fearful symmetry

After considering the whole poem, look specifically at the following points:

1 Why did Blake delete the stanza from line 13 to line 17?

2 This deletion leaves stanza 3 grammatically incomplete. Does this produce clumsiness, or incomprehensibility, or what?

3 One critic has suggested that the word 'feet' (line 12) acquires a special strength when the deletion leaves it as the last word of the stanza. Look again at how the sentence originally continued, and say whether you agree with the critic.

4 Discuss the relative merits of 'where' and 'what' (line 18); 'the arm', 'the grasp', 'the clasp' and 'dread grasp' (line 20); 'Dare' and 'Could' (line 21); 'form' and 'frame' (line 25).

2. *Additions to the First Draft*
On the opposite page of Blake's notebook appear the following
alternative version of the second stanza, all of it crossed out, and a
draft of an additional stanza:

Burnt in distant deeps or skies
The cruel fire of thine eyes
Could heart descend or wings aspire
What the hand dare sieze the. fire

~~dare he smile laugh~~
5 And ~~did he laugh~~ his work to see

~~ankle~~
~~What the shoulder what the knee~~
Dare
~~Did~~ he who made the lamb make thee
.When the stars threw down their spears
And waterd heaven with their tears

1 Note very carefully the detailed differences between this version
  of the second stanza and the earlier one. Does this version differ
  in its general emphasis? Why did Blake prefer his former version?
2 Does the appearance of the new draft stanza (presumably later
  than the First Draft) represent any change in Blake's subject
  matter or attitude?
3 Discuss the differences between 'laugh' and 'smile', 'ankle' and
  'shoulder', 'Did' and 'Dare'.

3. *Second Draft*

    Tyger Tyger burning bright
    In the forests of the night
    What Immortal hand & eye
    Dare frame thy fearful symmetry

    And what shoulder & what art
5 Could twist the sinews of thy heart
    And when thy heart began to beat
    What dread hand & what dread feet

    When the stars threw down their spears
    And water'd heaven with their tears
10 Did he smile his work to see
    Did he who made the lamb make thee

    Tyger Tyger burning bright
    In the forests of the night
    What immortal hand & eye
15 Dare frame thy fearful symmetry

1 Would you say that there had been any change in Blake's emphasis at this stage in his work on the poem?

2 The stanza which has become verse 3 in this Second Draft has had its lines rearranged since it first appeared as an addition to the First Draft. Is this an improvement?

3 Blake has now made up his mind between 'smile' and 'laugh', and between 'ankle' and 'shoulder'. What do these preferences suggest?

The Tyger

Tyger! Tyger! burning bright
In the forests of the night,
What immortal hand or eye
Could frame thy fearful symmetry?

5 In what distant deeps or skies
Burnt the fire of thine eyes?
On what wings dare he aspire?
What the hand dare sieze the fire?

And what shoulder, & what art,
10 Could twist the sinews of thy heart?
And when thy heart began to beat,
What dread hand? & what dread feet?

What the hammer? what the chain?
In what furnace was thy brain?
15 What the anvil? what dread grasp
Dare its deadly terrors clasp?

When the stars threw down their spears,
And water'd heaven with their tears,
Did he smile his work to see?
20 Did he who made the Lamb make thee?

Tyger! Tyger! burning bright
In the forests of the night,
What immortal hand or eye
Dare frame thy fearful symmetry?

1 What further shifts in meaning or emphasis, if any, are brought about by restoring some earlier stanzas?

2 Comment specially on the differences between this Final Version and the earlier versions of lines 5, 6, 7 and 13.

3 In connection with lines 17–18, is it relevant to know that Blake uses a similar idea elsewhere, as follows?

> Throw down thy sword and musket
> And run and embrace the meek peasant.
> (*The French Revolution*, lines 220–1)

The British soldiers thro' the thirteen states sent up a howl
Of anguish, threw their swords & muskets to the earth, & ran
From their encampments and dark castles, seeking where to hide
(*America*, Plate 13, lines 6–8)

The builder of Virginia throws his hammer down in fear.
(*America*, Plate 14, line 16)

B   Owen's 'Anthem for Doomed Youth'

1. *First Draft*

             passing
What ~~minute~~ bells for these who die so fast?
       ~~solemn~~
—Only the monstrous anger of our guns.
Let the majestic insults of their iron mouths
            requiem
Be as the ~~priest-words~~ of their burials.
5 Of choristers and holy music, none;
    Nor any voice of mourning, save the wail
The long-drawn wail of high far-sailing shells.
            to light
What candles may we hold ~~for~~ these lost? ~~souls?~~
—Not in the hands of boys, but in their eyes
  shine the ~~tapers~~   the holy ~~tapers~~ candles.
10 Shall / many ~~candles;~~ ~~shine;~~ ~~and I will~~ ~~light them.~~
       ~~holy~~ flames: to
Women's wide-spreaded arms shall be their wreaths,
And pallor of girls' cheeks shall be their palls.
           ~~mortal~~
Their flowers, the tenderness of ~~all~~ ~~men's~~ minds,
         ~~comrades'~~
         rough men's
    each slow
And ~~every~~ Dusk, a drawing-down of blinds.

Note:

(i) On the original manuscript are several pencilled amendments by
Siegfried Sassoon, to whom Owen showed this sonnet. These
have been omitted from the above transcript, since Owen seems
to have accepted none of the suggested improvements except the
change from 'our' (line 2) to the more impersonal 'the' in the
second and final drafts.

(ii) The word 'I' (line 10) is a doubtful reading. The original line
may have ended with 'light' preceded by an indecipherable word
of two syllables.

2. *Second Draft*

for
Anthem ~~to~~ Dead Youth

What passing-bells for you who die in herds?

the

—Only the monstrous anger of ~~more~~ guns!
—Only the stuttering rifles' rattled words
Can patter out your hasty orisons.

choirs

5 No chants for you, nor blams, nor wreaths, nor bells

shells

    Nor any voice of mourning, save the choirs,
And long-drawn sighs
~~The shrill demented choirs of~~ wailing shells;
    And bugles. calling for you from sad shires.

What candles may we hold to speed you all?
    Not in the hands of boys, but in their eyes
Shall S   ~~and gleams~~ our
~~Shall~~ shine ~~the~~ holy lights/ of ~~long~~ goodbyes.

must

The pallor of girls' brows ~~shall~~ be your pall;

~~broken simple frail~~

Your flowers, the tenderness of ~~mortal~~ minds,

~~pain white~~
~~grief wh innocent~~
comrades'

And each slow dusk, a drawing-down of blinds.

3. *Third Draft*

What passing-bells for these dumb-dying cattle?
    —Only the monstrous anger of more guns!
Only the stuttering rifles' rapid rattle
    Can patter out their hasty orisons.
5 No chants for them, nor wreaths, nor asphodels,
    Nor any voice of mourning save the choirs
The shrill demented choirs of wailing shells;
    And bugles calling for them from sad shires.

100

What candles may we hold to speed them all?
10   Not in the hands of boys, but in their eyes
Shall shine the holy gleams ·of their goodbyes.
        The pallor of girls' cheeks shall be their pall.
Their flowers the tenderness of silent minds
And each slow dusk a drawing-down of blinds.

4. Fourth Draft
Doomed
Anthem for ~~Dead~~ Youth
What passing bells for these who die as cattle?
    —Only the monstrous anger of the guns.
        Only the stuttering rifles' rapid rattle
Can patter out their hasty orisons.
        ~~music for all them~~   ~~nor~~ no   nor
5 No mockeries for them; ~~from~~ prayers ~~or~~ bells,
            now
        Nor any voice of mourning save the choirs,
                ented
The shrill ~~demonic~~ choirs of wailing shells;
                for them from sad
And bugles calling ~~sad across the~~ shires.

What candles may be held to speed them all?
10   Not in the hands of boys, but in their eyes
Shall shine the holy glimmers of goodbyes.
~~And~~ The pallor of girls' brows shall be their pall;
                silent patient
Their flowers the tenderness of ~~sweet white~~ minds,
And each slow dusk a drawing-down of blinds.

Is there any significant change in the general sense of the poem between
the first and last versions?

When do the metrical and rhyme schemes become fixed?

Work in detail through the drafts, either line by line or sentence by
sentence, to consider why Owen hesitated over certain parts, and how
he seems to have made his decisions.

Some particular points for consideration:

1 Certain words in the first draft ('our' (line 2), 'we' (line 8), 'comrades' (line 13) and the second draft (e.g. 'you' (line 1), 'your' (line 4), 'our' (line 11), etc.) are omitted from the third and fourth drafts. Why?

2 Why do you think Owen rejected the idea contained in line 11 of the first draft.

3 Discuss the change from 'every' to 'each slow' (first draft, last line); from 'gleams' (third draft, line 11) to 'glimmers' (fourth draft, line 11); from 'silent' (third draft, line 13) to 'patient' (fourth draft, line 13).

4 In the fourth draft, line 15, Owen first wrote 'No mockeries for them from prayers or bells', then contemplated changing 'mockeries' to 'music', and finally fixed on 'No mockeries for them; no prayers nor bells'. Discuss these three versions.

C   Dylan Thomas: 'Poem on his Birthday'

This section simply contains the final version, followed by a reproduction of the poet's worksheets.

Poem on his Birthday

In the mustardseed sun,
By full tilt river and switchback sea
Where the cormorants scud,
In his house on stilts high among beaks
5   And palavers of birds
This sandgrain day in the bent bay's grave
He celebrates and spurns
His driftwood thirty-fifth wind turned age;
Herons spire and spear.

10   Under and round him go
Flounders, gulls, on their cold, dying trails,
Doing what they are told,
Curlews aloud in the congered waves
Work at their ways to death,
15 And the rhymer in the long tongued room,
Who tolls his birthday bell,
Toils towards the ambush of his wounds;
Herons, steeple stemmed, bless.

In the thistledown fall,
20 He sings towards anguish; finches fly
In the claw tracks of hawks
On a seizing sky; small fishes glide
Through wynds and shells of drowned
Ship towns to pastures of otters. He
25   In his slant, racking house
And the hewn coils of his trade perceives
Herons walk in their shroud,

The livelong river's robe
Of minnows wreathing around their prayer;
30   And far at sea he knows,
Who slaves to his crouched, eternal end
        Under a serpent cloud,
Dolphins dive in their turnturtle dust,
        The rippled seals streak down
35 To kill and their own tide daubing blood
        Slides good in the sleek mouth.

        In a cavernous, swung
Wave's silence, wept white angelus knells.
        Thirty-five bells sing struck
40 On skull and scar where his loves lie wrecked,
        Steered by the falling stars.
And to-morrow weeps in a blind cage
        Terror will rage apart
Before chains break to a hammer flame
45   And love unbolts the dark

        And freely he goes lost
In the unknown, famous light of great
        And fabulous, dear God.
Dark is a way and light is a place,
50   Heaven that never was
Nor will be ever is always true,
        And, in that brambled void,
Plenty as blackberries in the woods
        The dead grow for His joy.

55   There he might wander bare
With the spirits of the horseshoe bay
        Or the stars' seashore dead,
Marrow of eagles, the roots of whales
        And wishbones of wild geese,
60 With blessed, unborn God and His Ghost,
        And every soul His priest,
Gulled and chanter in young Heaven's fold
        Be at cloud quaking peace,

But dark is a long way.
65 He, on the earth of the night, alone
    With all the living, prays,
Who knows the rocketing wind will blow
    The bones out of the hills,
And the scythed boulders bleed, and the last
70   Rage shattered waters kick
Masts and fishes to the still quick stars,
    Faithlessly unto Him

    Who is the light of old
And air shaped Heaven where souls grow wild
75   As horses in the foam:
Oh, let me midlife mourn by the shrined
    And druid herons' vows
The voyage to ruin I must run,
    Dawn ships clouted aground,
80 Yet, though I cry with tumbledown tongue,
    Count my blessings aloud:

    Four elements and five
Senses, and man a spirit in love
    Tangling through this spun slime
85 To his nimbus bell cool kingdom come
    And the lost, moonshine domes,
And the sea that hides his secret selves
    Deep in its black, base bones,
Lulling of spheres in the seashell flesh,
90   And this last blessing most,

    That the closer I move
To death, one man through his sundered hulks,
    The louder the sun blooms
And the tusked, ramshackling sea exults;
95   And every wave of the way
And gale I tackle, the whole world then,
    With more triumphant faith
Than ever was since the world was said,
    Spins its morning of praise,

100   I hear the bouncing hills
     Grow larked and greener at berry brown
          Fall and the dew larks sing
     Taller this thunderclap spring, and how
          More spanned with angels ride
105 The mansouled fiery islands! Oh,
          Holier then their eyes,
     And my shining men no more alone
          As I sail out to die.

DYLAN THOMAS

Poem On His Birthday

In the mustardseed sun,
By eely river and switchback sea
   where the cormorants scud,
In his house on stilts high among beaks
   And palavers of birds
This sandgrain day in the bent bay's grave
   He celebrates and spurns
His driftwood thirty fifth wind-turned age;
   Herons spire and spear.

   Under and round him go
Flounders, gulls, on their dying trails,
   Doing what they are told,
Curlews aloud in the congered waves
   Work at their ways to death,
And the rhymer ~~in~~ the long tongued room, ✓
   Who tolls his ~~birthday~~ bell,
Toils ~~~~ the ambush of his wounds;
~~In~~ ~~the~~ thistledown fall,
He sings towards anguish; finches fly
   In the claw tracks of hawks
On a ~~shambling~~ sky; small fishes glide
~~through the waters~~ of the drowned
   to the islands of otters. He
~~And~~ the hewn coils of his trade perceives
   Herons walk in their shroud,
       ~~~~dled
The ~~peopled~~ river's robe
Of minnows rippling around their prayer;
   And far at sea he knows,
Who slaves afraid to his fury and
   In a spiralling cloud,
Dolphins dive in their turnturtle pall,
   Seafoxes and seaowls
Taste the flesh of their death ~~moon~~ the trawled
Dales) ~~~~ as they pounce and mouth.

   Thirty five bellnotes ~~from~~

caves   muzzles
combes   gullet
scallops isle,
whorls.   an w.

• windings
wheels
oriels
domes
arches

£
{ 23   Passage
{ 161   passage
{ 424   outpace

eyelids
doors ✓

nets ✓
folds

gardens
orchards
islands
tithing,
townships

yards   a.
acres   +
moors
prairies
fabric
structures

184
7-60

towns
lantoya
parks
sweep
crafts
spots
lanes ✓
road ✓
walk
downs
nets
sands ✓

Poem On His Birthday

In the mustardseed sun,
By gulltilt river and switchback sea
Where the cormorants scud,
In his house on stilts high among beaks
And palavers of birds
This sandgrain day in the bent bay's grave
He celebrates and spurns
His driftwood thirty fifth wind turned age;
Herons spire and spear.

Under and round him go
Flounders, gulls, on their cold, dying trails,
Doing what they are told,
Curlews aloud in the congered waves
Work at their ways to death,
And the rhymer in the long tongued room,
Who tolls his birthday bell,
Toils towards the ambush of his wounds.
Herons, on one leg, bless.

In the thistledown fall
He sings towards anguish; finches glide   finch gives.
Through the eyes of the drowned
Towns to the island pastures of otters. He
In his winged, racking house
And the keen coils of his trade perceives
Herons walk in their shroud,

The livelong river's robe
Of minnows wreathing around their prayer;
And far at sea he knows,
Who slaves afraid to his deathless end
In a spiralling cloud,
Dolphins dive in their turnturtle dust,
The rippled seals streak down
To kill and their own tide daubing blood
Slides good in the sleek mouth.

_____
                gulls
Through the lanes of the drowned
Sea towns to pastures of otters. He   —
  •

                  deers

And far at sea he knows,
Who slaves afraid to his fiery end
In a spiralling cloud,
Dolphins dive in their turnturtle fall

The seaouls swoop & pounce   Dive, &
In green wom seafoul pounce

Seabears go killing down
And taste the flesh of their own death, salt
And good in the dark mouth

The flesh they pounce
Upon is the flesh of their own death, salt   bite
And good in the dark mouth.
                    that
And the fish was dived down
To kill, taste the flesh of their own salt   ✓
Death good in the dark mouth.

Seafoxes pouncing down   ✓

_____

thresh deep   awl
                              Crater mouth   for
sead.   death   'sor.   ⌣   awe
                                                   or
loom   moor
tower   moored
swingeing   more

112   animal
                         sleeking
        And the seals that sleek down
To kill, taste the flesh of their own salt raw unborn
        Death, good in the dark mouth.

                                          Low
Vas'   whales that dome down   oven

        Dolphins in their turnturtle fall dive deep
        And the seals that sleek down
To k   halm   ⭕

ball call crawl haul squall trawl wall hault   Eja in
caught drawn gorge horde howlm jaw law paw port sprr row
Sword tall YAWN
                                stencil   bull mill

                    109

At half his bible span,
A man of words who'd drag down the stars to his lyric oven,
He looks back at his years.

ᵟ   A lyrical man

At half his bible span,
A lyrical man ~~who could~~ who'd pull the stars
~~And~~ And the

And the ~~39~~ years ~~span~~ spinning back to the dark,

The dead ~~39~~ years ~~spinning~~ spinning back to the dark
gong,

The cocklesucked Thirty five

H   ransacked love

The ~~two~~ spent loves spinning back to the

Thirty five ways to death

Bygone love makes a sound
like ~~a bell~~
ball ducked in the foam
gong
Long gongs ducked in the foam deep

d
Keening
requiem
Jeremiad
dirge
sackcloth
coronach Koronah
a cypress bell
sacring bell
angelus

550
363
417

Thirty five ~~stages~~ to

Bygone love. ~~makes a sound~~ a cypress bell
~~Sw~~ Swung in fanes of the foam
chantries of
ministers

Knelled
Swung in sea ministers

5 WRITING POETRY

Writing your own poetry is really a topic for another book[1] although probably the best way to learn to write poetry is to write it. However, the attempt to write can be a further means of developing insight into the work of more established poets. In this chapter, we suggest three approaches which could start you writing in the hope that this will be of value in itself and also in your critical response to other poems.

A Through Subject Matter

In Question 1 on page 11, we asked 'Must poetry have a special subject matter?' Our own view is that there are no limits to themes appropriate for poetry, although it has to be faced that poems about experiments in physics are less common than those about love. (Why?)

The appropriateness of the subject depends rather upon the ability of the writer to recognise and to communicate the uniqueness of what he has experienced. To one man, a child laughing and swinging on a rope tied to a lamp-post in the dusk could suggest echoes of his own childhood; to another, the exuberance of his own son; to another, a potential road-hazard; to another, a child laughing and swinging on a rope tied to a lamp-post in the dusk.

To recognise the distinctiveness of the way each individual perceives, you could use some of the following as stimuli, and write (in prose or verse) whatever comes into your head—disjointedly, if you wish: a landscape painting, a portrait, an abstract painting; a piece of instrumental music; these words—heron, anguish, priest, joy, ivy; a waste-paper basket; lastly, if possible, an incident lasting about five minutes which two of you improvise for the others. Now read some of the reactions back to one another to compare the diversity of response.

Try now to examine your own experience and to recognise its uniqueness if you can. This is obviously difficult without localising

---

1 In fact, it *is* the topic of two books which we recommend:
   Ted Hughes: *Poetry in the Making*, Faber.
   Brian Powell: *English Through Poetry Writing*, Heinemann.

certain areas; some of the following might provide points from which poems might grow:

A very early memory of pain; of relief; of insecurity.

A moment when you knew *at the time* (not merely in retrospect) that you were intensely happy.

A time of extreme quiet or stillness.

An experience or relationship which might be described as exploratory—one which left you with greater insight into yourself or other people.

An object or place which has been familiar to you throughout your life.

These suggestions are made very tentatively, in that shaping your choice too far is precisely what we want to avoid. It would naturally be preferable to work from a subject which really makes you want to write, since poetry cannot be written to order.

B Through Images

The Thought-Fox
I imagine this midnight moment's forest:
Something else is alive
Beside the clock's loneliness
And this blank page where my fingers move.

5 Through the window I see no star:
Something more near
Though deeper within darkness
Is entering the loneliness:

Cold, delicately as the dark snow,
10 A fox's nose touches twig, leaf;
Two eyes serve a movement, that now
And again now, and now, and now

Sets neat prints into the snow
Between trees, and warily a lame
15 Shadow lags by stump and in hollow
Of a body that is bold to come

Across clearings, an eye,
A widening deepening greenness,
Brilliantly, concentratedly,
20 Coming about its own business

Till, with a sudden sharp hot stink of fox
It enters the dark hole of the head.
The window is starless still; the clock ticks,
The page is printed.

TED HUGHES

This poem provides a useful way-in to the writing of poetry because here we can eavesdrop on the writer's thought sequence as he records the mental image of this fox. We are given the illusion of seeing the poem write itself. It is not an 'animal' poem as much as a poem about writing poetry.

Ted Hughes's way of thinking and the image he creates of the fox as the words gradually make up the picture may give you a clue as to how to start a piece of your own writing. You may be able to develop a strong mental image from your own experience: a dream? a childhood fear? a place which has associations for you? a relationship with someone which has been, or is, of special importance to you?

.   .   .

From ways of thinking to ways of looking—thirteen ways, in fact, of looking at a familiar sight.

Thirteen Ways of Looking at a Blackboard

I
The blackboard is clean.
The master must be coming.

II
The vigilant mosquito bites on a rising pitch.
The chalk whistles over the blackboard.

III
Among twenty silent children
The only moving thing
Is the chalk's white finger.

IV
O young white cricketers,
Aching for the greensward,
Do you not see how my moving hand
Whitens the black board?

V
A man and a child
Are one.
A man and a child and a blackboard
Are three.

VI
Some wield their sticks of chalk
Like torches in dark rooms.
I make up my blackboard
Like the face of an actor.

VII
I was of three minds
Like a room
In which there are three blackboards.

VIII

I dream.
I am an albino.

IX

I wake.
I forget a word.
The chalk snaps on the blackboard.

X

Twenty silent children
Staring at the blackboard.
On one wall of each of twenty nurseries
The light has gone out.

XI

He ambles along the white rocks of Dover,
Crushing pebbles with black boots.
He is a small blackboard
Writing on chalk.

XII

It is the Christmas holidays.
The white snow lies in the long black branches.
The black board
In the silent schoolroom
Perches on two stubby branches.

XIII

The flesh that is white
Wastes over the bones that are chalk,
Both in the day
And through the black night.

PETER REDGROVE

You may want to spend some time thinking about this poem or
discussing it with the rest of the group, but do not lose sight of the

simple point that may help you with your own writing: Peter Redgrove has seen the possibilities in an everyday object for developing a series of images. Perhaps this is a place at which you could start, too. The poet sees things in new perspectives; objects suggest ideas and comparisons; objects become symbols. Could you imitate this poem with an object of your own choosing? The following things can be looked at in many ways and may suggest ideas to you: a clockface, a piece of coal, a mirror, a lighted lamp, a stream, a wall.

．　　　　．　　　　．

Frequently, a poem can grow out of the sudden recognition of a likeness between two things. What is the common quality, for example, between the two parts of the comparison in each of the following short poems?

(*a*) **In a Station of the Metro**
The apparition of these faces in the crowd;
Petals on a wet, black bough.
EZRA POUND

(*b*) **Fog**
The fog comes
on little cat feet.

It sits looking
over harbour and city
5 on silent haunches
and then moves on.
CARL SANDBURG

(*c*) **Winter**
The winter trees like great sweep's brushes
Poke up from deep earth, black and bare,
Suddenly stir, and shake a crowd
Of sooty rooks into the air.
L. A. G. STRONG

You might now try writing a piece which, like these, relies mainly on developing a single image.

C   Through Form

If you have attempted to write poetry before, perhaps only recently as a result of this chapter, you will have realised that the form of your poem depends directly on what you want to say. You may have discovered already that one pattern appeals to you more than another, that you prefer, say, free verse to sonnets or couplet poetry. However keen you may be on one style of writing, it is a good idea to give yourself some practice in several different forms so that, on those occasions when you experience something that you really want to write about, you have a certain amount of freedom to choose the most appropriate form for that particular subject. On such occasions, you could use the Index and the Glossary of this book to help you find out the technical information that you need. Meanwhile, here are three forms which we would encourage you to attempt.

1. Haiku

Haiku poetry is Japanese in origin. As you will see from the example, this form, because it consists of only three lines, cannot incorporate a lot of detail: what detail there is must be significant and important to the description. The haiku poet has to choose his words with great care because he is using so few; his poems may suggest a scene or incident, they may create an atmosphere, they may express a person's feelings, or they may do several of these things simultaneously. The only technical rule governing the haiku form is that the poem should consist of seventeen syllables, arranged 5, 7, 5 on the three lines. The rhymes in this example are an optional extra:

City People
Townsfolk, it is plain—
Carrying red maple leaves
In the homebound train.
        MEISETSU (*trans.* H. G. HENDERSON)[1]

Try it yourself.

---

[1] Harold G. Henderson: *An Introduction to Haiku*, Doubleday Anchor.

2. Free Verse

Have another look, for examples, at D. H. Lawrence's *Bat* on page 54 or T. S. Eliot's *Rhapsody on a Windy Night* on page 160.

In what sense is free verse 'free'?

What controls the shape of a free verse poem?

Once you have discussed these points you could usefully attempt some free verse writing of your own.

3. Sonnet

You will find some useful technical information in the Glossary. Because the sonnet is one of the most demanding forms it is also one of the most satisfying to achieve. When you have become familiar with the metre and rhyme schemes, read through some of the sonnets on pages 41, 51, 57, 72, 73, 99–101, 136, 142, 163, 187, 195, 197 and 201.

To what sort of subject matter do you think the form especially appropriate?

Now experiment yourself.

6 WHAT IS POETRY?

When he was asked that question, Dr. Samuel Johnson replied: 'Why, Sir, it is much easier to say what it is not. We all KNOW what light is; but it is not easy to *tell* what it is.' Probably you have sometimes felt unsure whether a particular piece of writing was a poem or not, whether there could be prose poems, and so on. The purpose of this chapter is to try to help you to discuss such questions more profitably, by bringing together some answers given by writers for you to examine and by suggesting a method of dealing with the problems of definition. Section G provides a number of pieces of writing against which you can test your conclusions.

A Poetry Is . . .

The elevated expression of elevated thought or feeling in metrical form.
(*The Concise Oxford Dictionary*)

Prose = words in their best order. Poetry = the BEST words in the best order. (S. T. COLERIDGE)

All metaphor is poetry. (G. K. CHESTERTON)

Simile and metaphor [are] things inessential to poetry. (A. E. HOUSMAN)

Poetry is not the thing said, but a way of saying it. (A. E. HOUSMAN)

Poetry should be great and unobtrusive, a thing which enters into one's soul, and does not startle it or amaze it with itself, but with its subject.
(JOHN KEATS)

> The great end
> Of poesy, that it should be a friend
> To soothe the cares, and lift the thoughts of man. (JOHN KEATS)

[Poetry is] the suggestion, by the imagination, of noble grounds for the noble emotions. (JOHN RUSKIN)

Genuine poetry is conceived and composed in the soul.
(MATTHEW ARNOLD)

Poetry [involves] criticism of life. . . . But for supreme poetical success more is required than the powerful application of ideas to life . . . [i.e.] the high seriousness which comes from absolute sincerity.
(MATTHEW ARNOLD)

Poetry is generally esteemed the highest form of literature.
(A. E. HOUSMAN)

Is 'E= Mc²' an elevated thought? If not, would it become poetry if expressed in metre, thus: 'E equals Mc² is really true'? If not, why not?

Does a poem *have* to be elevated and elevating? Couldn't one write a poem in ordinary language about an ordinary state of mind or a commonplace occurrence? (Can you think of an example of such a poem?) Could it be depressing rather than elevating to read?

Is prose just any old words put into 'the best order'?

Does Housman (in the first remark of his quoted) contradict Chesterton?

Does the first remark quoted from Keats contradict the second from Housman?

In what sense (if any) could poetry be 'composed in the soul'?

Does the second remark quoted from Matthew Arnold imply that even the best comic verse is not poetry?

Is poetry a higher form of literature than (say) the novel or prose drama? If so, why, and in what sense of 'higher'?

Those are some questions you could ask yourself about the first batch of quotations. From here on you will largely be left to raise your own objections to the views you are presented with and to draw your own conclusions.[1]

B How Poetry Works

> Meaning is of the intellect, poetry is not. . . . Poetry [is] more physical than intellectual. . . . To transfuse emotion—not to transmit thought but to set up in the reader's sense a vibration corresponding to what was felt by the writer—is the peculiar function of poetry.
>
> (A. E. Housman)

> True ease in writing comes from art, not chance,
> As those move easiest who have learn'd to dance.   (Alexander Pope)

[1] For further reading on the subject of this chapter, see:
English Critical Texts, ed. D. J. Enright and Ernst de Chickera (Oxford University Press).
The Poet Speaks, ed. Peter Orr (Routledge and Kegan Paul).
Poets on Poetry, ed. Charles Norman (Free Press; Collier-Macmillan).
Modern Poets on Modern Poetry, ed. James Scully (Fontana Books).
'On "What Is a Poem?" ', an article by C. L. Stevenson in *The Philosophical Review*, Vol. LXCI, July 1957.

The only way of expressing emotion in a work of art is by finding an 'objective correlative', in other words, a set of objects, a situation, a chain of events which shall be the formula of that particular emotion; such that when the external facts, which must terminate in sensory experience, are given, the emotion is immediately evoked.

(T. S. Eliot)

It is the poet's task to find, to invent, the special language which will alone be capable of expressing his personality and feelings. Such a language must make use of symbols: what is so special, so fleeting and so vague, cannot be conveyed by direct statement or description, but only by a succession of words, of images, which will serve to suggest it to the reader.   (Edmund Wilson, explaining Mallarmé's ideas)

Poetry awakens and enlarges the mind itself by rendering it the receptacle of a thousand unapprehended combinations of thought. Poetry lifts the veil from the hidden beauty of the world, and makes familiar objects be as if they were not familiar. . . . The great instrument of moral good is the imagination; and poetry administers to the effect by acting upon the cause.   (P. B. Shelley)

When a poet's mind is perfectly equipped for its work it is constantly amalgamating disparate experience; the ordinary man's experience is chaotic, irregular, fragmentary. The latter falls in love or reads Spinoza, and these two experiences have nothing to do with each other, or with the noise of the typewriter, or the smell of cooking; in the mind of the poet these experiences are always forming new wholes.   (T. S. Eliot)

C   Poets

The three quotations which follow express a romantic point of view, and it should be pointed out that many poets do not think of themselves in this way.

Pope would not be decoyed from his path by any will-o'-the-wisp of Science, interest in human nature, the wish to reform, or other poetry-wrecking influences. . . . Verses written by a person who is not a poet, no matter how worthy his motives may be, are not poetry.

(Edith Sitwell)

A poet is more delicately organised than other men, and sensible to pain and pleasure, both his own and that of others, in a degree unknown to them. . . . Poets are the hierophants of an unapprehended inspiration. . . . Poets are the unacknowledged legislators of the world.

(P. B. Shelley)

We are the music makers,
We are the dreamers of dreams,
Wandering by lonely sea-breakers,
And sitting by desolate streams;—

World-losers and world-forsakers,
On whom the pale moon gleams:
We are the movers and shakers
Of the world for ever, it seems.   (A. W. E. O'SHAUGHNESSY)

Do *you* think poets are a select few, a gifted minority? Compare pianists, athletes, short-story writers, and so on.

D   How Poetry is Written

Poetry is not like reasoning, a power to be exerted according to the determination of the will. A man cannot say, 'I will compose poetry'. The greatest poet even cannot say it; for the mind in creation is as a fading coal, which some invisible influence, like an inconstant wind, awakens to transitory brightness; this power arises from within . . . and the conscious portions of our natures are unprophetic either of its approach or its departure. . . . When composition begins, inspiration is already on the decline, and the most glorious poetry that has ever been communicated to the world is probably a feeble shadow of the original conceptions of the poet.   (P. B. SHELLEY)

I get an idea, a sort of germ comes, and if that comes I know the poem will be finished. But it may take me weeks and weeks of brooding and thinking about this exciting idea, and then suddenly the poem will arrive; but it takes a long period of gestation; then once that birthpoint has been reached the thing is written quickly; but then comes the working over and that's a long process.   (THOMAS BLACKBURN)

If poetry comes not as naturally as the leaves to a tree, it had better not come at all.   (JOHN KEATS)

Poetry is the spontaneous overflow of powerful feelings: it takes its origin from emotion recollected in tranquillity: the emotion is contemplated till, by a species of reaction, the tranquillity gradually disappears, and an emotion, kindred to that which was before the subject of contemplation, is gradually produced, and does itself actually exist in the mind. . . . But the emotion . . . is qualified by various pleasures, so that in describing any passions whatsoever, which are voluntarily described, the mind will, upon the whole, be in a state of enjoyment.
     (WILLIAM WORDSWORTH)

To what extent do these accounts agree with each other? Do they fit *your* experience of writing poetry? How would *you* describe the process?

Why, do you think, did Wordsworth add the sentence beginning 'But the emotion'?

E   Two Summaries

Here are two overall views of the nature of poetry, poets and the process of composition for you to compare and discuss.

> What is a poet? To whom does he address himself? And what language is to be expected from him? He is a man speaking to men: a man, it is true, endowed with more lively sensibility, more enthusiasm and tenderness, who has a greater knowledge of human nature, and a more comprehensive soul, than are supposed to be common among mankind. . . . The Poet is chiefly distinguished from other men by a greater promptness to think and feel without immediate external excitement, and a greater power in expressing such thoughts and feelings as are produced in him in that manner. But these passions and thoughts and feelings are the general passions and thoughts and feelings of men. And with what are they connected? Undoubtedly with our moral sentiments and animal sensations, and with the causes which excite these; with the operations of the elements, and the appearances of the visible universe; with storm and sunshine, with the revolutions of the seasons, with cold and heat, with loss of friends and kindred, with injuries and resentments, gratitude and hope, with fear and sorrow. These, and the like, are the sensations and objects which the Poet describes, as they are the sensations of other men, and the objects which interest them. The Poet thinks and feels in the spirit of human passions. How, then, can his language differ in any material degree from that of all other men who feel vividly and see clearly? . . . In order to excite rational sympathy, he must express himself as other men express themselves.[1]   (WILLIAM WORDSWORTH)

> The poem is a statement in words about a human experience. Words are primarily conceptual, but through use, and because human experience is not purely conceptual, they have acquired connotations of feeling. The poet makes his statement in such a way as to employ both concept and connotation as efficiently as possible. The poem is good in so far as it

[1] Gerard Manley Hopkins remarked that the language of poetry 'should be the current language, to any degree heightened and unlike itself, but not (I mean normally: passing freaks and graces are another thing) an obsolete one'.

makes a defensible, rational statement about a given human experience
. . . and at the same time communicates the emotion which ought to be
motivated by that rational understanding of that experience.

(YVOR WINTERS)

F   The Meaning of Words

It may help us to think more clearly about the meaning of the words
poetry, *poem*, *poet*, *poetic*, etc., if we pause for a few moments to consider
the way in which words in general mean what they do, since there is no
reason to suppose that the words we are discussing operate differently
from all others.

If we label someone as 'neurotic', what set of characteristics are we
attributing to him? Perhaps he is nervous, perhaps he has a tic, perhaps
he bursts into a temper at the slightest provocation, perhaps he is
unstable and can't be depended on even in the most ordinary situations,
and so on.   None of these things is a defining characteristic of his being
neurotic; he could do without one or more of them and be neurotic in
spite of it. But is there a definite set of characteristics which make him
neurotic? Who could make such a list? And who could be sure that it
was a complete list (of the criteria he himself implicitly employed) even
if he did? Could he be sure that there were no other characteristics the
addition of which would make us more likely to call a person neurotic—
characteristics which, if added, would add some weight to tip the scales
in favour of his being called neurotic? Many times there is no such
definite number of characteristics on the list. To assign a definite number
is to construct an artificially simple verbal situation, often not found in
actual word-usage. Who can list how many there are in the group of
characteristics the presence of which (or of a majority of which) makes
us call someone 'intelligent'?

But how did this whole unfortunate situation arise? Don't we know
what we mean by our own words?

We do attach meanings to words—we give them meanings, otherwise
they would be mere noises. But the meanings we give are not clear and
definite, only enough so to suit our practical purposes, and sometimes
hardly even that. We know roughly what characteristics we have in
mind when we give a noise a designation, but we do not know as a rule
exactly which ones we would consider essential and which we could do
without. We use a word, and we have a rather indefinite group of
characteristics in mind when we use it, and we let it go at that.

'Don't the words really *have* more precise meanings, even though we
don't know them?' The answer should now be obvious. Words have

meanings only because we have *given* them meanings, otherwise they would be noises or pen-marks. And they have only *as much* meaning as we give them, no more. If the meaning we give them suffers from the drawbacks outlined above, then the meaning they *have* suffers from those drawbacks, since this is their only source of income. We cannot speak of the meaning as being 'really clear, if only we could discover it—what is gold really?' The moon has no more light than it reflects from the sun.[1]

It should not be difficult to see how that analysis applies to *poetry*, *poetic*, etc. However, beware of overstating the point Hospers is making. He isn't saying that it's impossible to define words at all. Most words may be vague, but within the limits of their (natural and inevitable) vagueness it is certainly possible to say what they mean; after all, if this were not so words would be of no use at all, and we shouldn't be able to tell (as we certainly can) when a word is being used wrongly or instead of another.

> But now a new complication descends upon us. If 'X' is defined in terms of characteristics A and B, then we must ask what A and B are defined in terms of. A is defined in terms of F, G, H, and B in terms of I, J, K. Then what are F, G, H, I, J and K defined in terms of? Well, F is defined in terms of M, N, O . . . But we shall soon run out of letters of the alphabet, and the point is becoming painfully clear.[2]

To apply these considerations to our present concern, if 'X' is the word *poetry*, what are the A, B, etc., in terms of which you would now define 'X'? You will remember that some answers suggested by famous writers are 'being elevated in thought and expression', 'being metaphorical', and 'working through suggestion'. What answers would you give?

And now how would you define the F, G, H, etc., that you have referred to in your answer? (For example, what *is* metaphor? What does rhythm consist in? How does suggestion differ from statement? How does feeling differ from thought?) You might be able to compare your definitions of some terms with those offered at the end of this book, and those in other glossaries.

John Hospers: *An Introduction to Philosophical Analysis*, 1st Edition, Chapter 1, Routledge and Kegan Paul, Ltd.

Ibid.

G Further Examples

The passages which follow have been specially selected to provide
opportunities to put to the test and perhaps reconsider whatever
conclusions you have reached about the nature of poetry. However,
they may also be regarded as further opportunities to practise critical
skills. The names of the authors are withheld, since they might
prejudice reactions. Information about authorship, and, in the case of
one example, some further information, may be found on page 225.
Do not turn to that page before you have arrived at judgements on the
passages; to do so would detract from the usefulness and the interest
of the exercise.

.   .   .

(a) In a coign of the cliff between lowland and highland,
    At the sea-down's edge between windward and lee,
  Walled round with rocks as an inland island,
    The ghost of a garden fronts the sea.
5 A girdle of brushwood and thorn encloses
    The steep square slope of the blossomless bed
  Where the weeds that grew green from the graves of its roses
        Now lie dead.

  The fields fall southward, abrupt and broken,
10   To the low last edge of the long lone land.
  If a step should sound or a word be spoken,
    Would a ghost not rise at the strange guest's hand?
  So long have the grey bare walks lain guestless,
    Through branches and briars if a man make way,
15 He shall find no life but the sea-wind's, restless
        Night and day.

.   .   .

(b) Two principles in human nature reign;
    Self-love, to urge, and Reason, to restrain;
    Nor this a good, nor that a bad we call,
    Each works its end, to move or govern all;
5 And to their proper operation still,
    Ascribe all good; to their improper, ill.

Self-love, the spring of motion, acts the soul;
Reason's comparing balance rules the whole.
Man, but for that, no action could attend,
10 And but for this, were active to no end:
Fix'd like a plant on his peculiar spot,
To draw nutrition, propagate, and rot;
Or, meteor-like, flame lawless through the void,
Destroying others, by himself destroy'd.

. . .

(c) The Strange Case of the Lovelorn Letter Writer

Dear Miss Dix, I am a young lady of Scandinavian origin, and I am
in a quandary.
I am not exactly broody, but I am kind of pondery.
I got a twenty-five waist and a thirty-five bust,
And I am going with a chap whose folks are very upper-crust.
5 He is the intellectual type, which I wouldn't want to disparage,
Because I understand they often ripen into love after marriage,
But here I am all set
For dalliance,
And what do I get?
10 Shilly-shalliance.
Just when I think he's going to disrobe me with his eyes,
He gets up off the davenport and sighs.
Every time I let down my hair,
He starts talking to himself or the little man who isn't there.
15 Every time he ought to be worrying about me,
Why, he's worrying about his mother, that's my mother-in-law
to be,
And I say let's burn that bridge when we come to it, and he says
don't I have any sin sense,
His uncle and her live in incense.
Well, with me that's fine,
20 Let them go to their church and I'll go to mine.
But no, that's not good enough for Mr. Conscience and his mental
indigestion,
He's got to find two answers for every question.
If a man is a man, a girl to him is a girl, if I correctly rememma,
But to him I am just a high pathetical dilemma.

25 What I love him in spite of
   Is, a girl wants a fellow to go straight ahead like a locomotive and
      he is more like a loco-might-of.
   Dear Miss Dix, I surely need your advice and solace.
   It's like I was in love with Henry Wallace.
   Well, while I eagerly await your reply I'm going down to the river
      to pick flowers. I'll get some rosemary if I can't find a camellia.
30 Yours truly, Ophelia.

                    .   .   .

(d) Under that porch, where she had sat when Heaven
    In its mercy brought her to that peaceful spot,
            She passed again,
    And the old church received her in its quiet shade.
5   Oh! it is hard
    To take to heart the lesson that such deaths will teach,
            But let no man
    Reject it, for it is one that all must learn
    And is a mighty, universal Truth.
10 When Death strikes down the innocent and young,
    For every fragile form from which he lets
    The panting spirit free, a hundred virtues rise,
    In shapes of mercy, charity, and love,
    To walk the world and bless it. Of every tear
15 That sorrowing mortals shed on such green graves,
    Some good is born, some gentler nature comes.

                    .   .   .

(e) Those who have a father
        Love him while you may,
    For we wish with all our hearts
        That ours was here today;
5   A heart of gold stopped beating,
        Two laughing eyes at rest,
    God broke our hearts to prove
        He only takes the best;
    For what it meant to lose him
10   No-one will ever know;
    Love in death should let us see
        What love in life should always be.

                    .   .   .

(*f*) The snail pushes through a green night, for the grass is heavy with
water and meets over the bright path he makes, where rain has
darkened the earth's dark. He moves in a wood of desire, pale
antlers barely stirring as he hunts. I cannot tell what power is at
work, drenched there with purpose, knowing nothing. What is a
snail's fury? All I think is that if later I parted the blades above
the tunnel and saw the thin trail of broken white across litter,
I would never have imagined the slow passion to that deliberate
progress.

.   .   .

(*g*)   go(perpe)go
                             (tu)to(al
                             adve

                             nturin
      5   g p
                             article

                             s of s
                             ini
                             sterd
     10   exte

                             ri)go to(ty)the(om
                             nivorou salways lugbrin
                             g ingseekfindlosin g
                             motilities
     15   are)go to

                             the
                             ant
                             (al
                             ways

     20   alingwaysing)
                             go to the ant thou go
                             (inging)

                             to the
                             ant, thou ant-

     25   eater

.   .   .

(h) Michael Henshard's Will

That Elizabeth-Jane Farfrae be not told of my death, or made to grieve on account of me.

And that I be not buried in consecrated ground.

And that no sexton be asked to toll the bell.

And that nobody is wished to see my dead body.

5 And that no mourners walk behind me at my funeral.

And that no flowers be planted on my grave.

And that no man remember me.

To this I put my name.

PART TWO

A SINGLE POEMS

A.1 Musée Des Beaux Arts

About suffering they were never wrong,
The Old Masters: how well they understood
Its human position; how it takes place
While someone else is eating or opening a window or just walking
    dully along;
5 How, when the aged are reverently, passionately waiting
For the miraculous birth, there always must be
Children who did not specially want it to happen, skating
On a pond at the edge of the wood:
They never forgot
10 That even the dreadful martyrdom must run its course
Anyhow in a corner, some untidy spot
Where the dogs go on with their doggy life and the torturer's
    horse
Scratches its innocent behind on a tree.

In Brueghel's *Icarus*, for instance: how everything turns away
15 Quite leisurely from the disaster; the ploughman may
Have heard the splash, the forsaken cry,
But for him it was not an important failure; the sun shone
As it had to on the white legs disappearing into the green
Water; and the expensive delicate ship that must have seen
20 Something amazing, a boy falling out of the sky,
Had somewhere to get to and sailed calmly on.

W. H. AUDEN

A.2 Psalm 126

When the Lord turned again the captivity of Zion, then were we like unto them that dream.

Then was our mouth filled with laughter, and our tongue with joy.

Then said they among the heathen: 'The Lord hath done great things for them.'

Yea, the Lord hath done great things for us already, whereof we rejoice.

Turn our captivity, O Lord, as the rivers in the south.

They that sow in tears shall reap in joy.

He that now goeth on his way weeping, and beareth forth good seed, shall doubtless come again with joy, and bring his sheaves with him.

A.3 I measure every grief I meet

I measure every grief I meet
   With analytic eyes;
I wonder if it weighs like mine,
   Or has an easier size.

5 I wonder if they bore it long
   Or did it just begin—
I could not tell the date of mine,
   It feels so old a pain.

I wonder if it hurts to live,
10   And if they have to try,
And whether—could they choose between—
   It would not be to die.

I note that some—gone patient long—
   At length renew their smile:
15 An imitation of a light
   That has too little oil.

I wonder if when years have piled,
  Some thousands, on the harm
That hurt them early, such a lapse
20   Could give them any balm.

Or would they go on aching still
  Through centuries of nerve,
Enlightened to a larger pain
  In contrast with the love.

25 The grieved are many, I am told;
  There is the various cause;
Death is but one and comes but once
  And only nails the eyes.

There's grief of want, and grief of cold—
30   A sort they call 'despair';
There's banishment from native eyes
  In sight of native air.

And though I may not guess the kind
  Correctly, yet to me
35 A piercing comfort it affords
  In passing Calvary,

To note the fashions of the cross,
  And how they're mostly worn,
Still fascinated to presume
40   That some are like my own.
                  EMILY DICKINSON

A.4 Holy Sonnet XIV

Batter my heart, three person'd God; for, you
As yet but knock, breathe, shine, and seek to mend;
That I may rise, and stand, o'erthrow me, and bend
Your force, to break, blow, burn and make me new.
5 I, like an usurp'd town, to another due,
Labour to admit you, but Oh, to no end,
Reason your viceroy in me, me should defend,
But is captiv'd, and proves weak or untrue.
Yet dearly I love you, and would be loved fain,
10 But am betroth'd unto your enemy:
Divorce me, untie, or break that knot again,
Take me to you, imprison me, for I
Except you enthrall me, never shall be free,
Nor ever chaste, except you ravish me.

JOHN DONNE

A.5 A Hymn to God the Father

Wilt thou forgive that sin, where I begun,
    Which is my sin, though it were done before?
Wilt thou forgive those sins through which I run
    And do run still, though still I do deplore?
5   When thou hast done, thou hast not done,
            For, I have more.

Wilt thou forgive that sin, by which I've won
    Others to sin, and made my sin their door?
Wilt thou forgive that sin which I did shun
10   A year or two, but wallowed in a score?
        When thou hast done, thou hast not done,
            For I have more.

I have a sin of fear that when I have spun
    My last thread, I shall perish on the shore;
15 Swear by thy self that at my death, thy Son
        Shall shine as he shines now, and heretofore;
            And having done that, thou hast done,
                I fear no more.

JOHN DONNE

A.6 Blue Umbrellas

'The thing that makes a blue umbrella with its tail—
How do you call it?' you ask. Poorly and pale
Comes my answer. For all I can call it is peacock.

Now that you go to school, you will learn how we call
5   all sorts of things;
How we mar great works by our mean recital.
You will learn, for instance, that Head Monster is not
    the gentleman's accepted title;
The blue-tailed eccentrics will be merely peacocks;
10   the dead bird will no longer doze
Off till tomorrow's lark, for the letter has killed him.
The dictionary is opening, the gay umbrellas close.

Oh our mistaken teachers!—
It was not a proper respect for words that we need,
15 But a decent regard for things, those older creatures
    and more real.
Later you may even resort to writing verse
To prove the dishonesty of names and their black greed—
To confess your ignorance, to expiate your crime,
20   seeking one spell to lift another curse.
Or you may, more commodiously, spy on your children,
    busy discoverers,
Without the dubious benefit of rhyme.

D. J. Enright

A.7 'Out, Out—'

The buzz saw snarled and rattled in the yard
And made dust and dropped stove-length sticks of wood,
Sweet-scented stuff when the breeze drew across it.
And from there those that lifted eyes could count
5 Five mountain ranges one behind the other
Under the sunset far into Vermont.
And the saw snarled and rattled, snarled and rattled,
As it ran light, or had to bear a load.
And nothing happened: day was all but done.
10 Call it a day, I wish they might have said
To please the boy by giving him the half hour
That a boy counts so much when saved from work.
His sister stood beside them in her apron
To tell them 'Supper'. At the word, the saw,
15 As if to prove saws knew what supper meant,
Leaped out at the boy's hand, or seemed to leap—
He must have given the hand. However it was,
Neither refused the meeting. But the hand!
The boy's first outcry was a rueful laugh,
20 As he swung toward them holding up the hand
Half in appeal, but half as if to keep
The life from spilling. Then the boy saw all—
Since he was old enough to know, big boy
Doing a man's work, though a child at heart—
25 He saw all spoiled. 'Don't let him cut my hand off—
The doctor, when he comes. Don't let him, sister!'
So. But the hand was gone already.
The doctor put him in the dark of ether.
He lay and puffed his lips out with his breath.
30 And then—the watcher at his pulse took fright.
No one believed. They listened at his heart.
Little—less—nothing!—and that ended it.
No more to build on there. And they, since they
Were not the one dead, turned to their affairs.

ROBERT FROST

A.8 Conversation Piece

By moonlight
At midnight,
Under the vines,
A hotel chair
5 Settles down moodily before the headlines
Of a still-folded evening newspaper.

The other chair
Of the pair
Lies on its back,
10 Stiff as in pain,
Having been overturned with an angry crack;
And there till morning, alas, it must remain.

On the terrace
No blood-trace,
15 No sorry glitter
Of a knife, nothing:
Not even the fine-torn fragments of a letter
Or the dull gleam of a flung-off wedding-ring.

Still stable
20 On the table
Two long-stemmed glasses,
One full of drink,
Watch how the rat among the vines passes
And how the moon trembles on the crag's brink.

ROBERT GRAVES

A.9 Paddington Canal

A mocking mirror, the black water turns
tall houses upside down, makes learned men
walk on their heads in squares of burning light;
lovers like folded bats hang in kiss,
5 swaying as if a breeze could sever them.
The barges, giant sea-birds fast asleep,
lie on the surface, moored and motionless;
then, drowning gently, are drawn down to join
the sunken lovers and the acrobats.
10 Out of the grim dimensions of a street
slowly I see another landscape grow
downwards into a lost reality;
a magic mirror, the black water tells
of a reversed Atlantis wisely built
15 to catch and to transform
the wasted substance of our daily acts,
accommodate our mad and lovely doubles
in a more graceful city timelessly.

MICHAEL HAMBURGER

A.10 At Castle Boterel

As I drive to the junction of lane and highway,
    And the drizzle bedrenches the waggonette,
I look behind at the fading byway,
    And see on its slope, now glistening wet,
5   Distinctly yet

Myself and a girlish form benighted
    In dry March weather. We climb the road
Beside a chaise. We had just alighted
    To ease the sturdy pony's load
10   When he sighed and slowed.

What we did as we climbed, and what we talked of
    Matters not much, nor to what it led,—
Something that life will not be balked of
    Without rude reason till hope is dead,
15   And feeling fled.

140

It filled but a minute. But was there ever
    A time of such quality, since or before,
In that hill's story? To one mind never,
    Though it has been climbed, foot-swift, foot-sore,
20   By thousands more.

Primaeval rocks form the road's steep border,
    And much have they faced there, first and last,
Of the transitory in Earth's long order;
    But what they record in colour and cast
25   Is—that we two passed.

And to me, though Time's unflinching rigour,
    In mindless rote, has ruled from sight
The substance now, one phantom figure
    Remains on the slope, as when that night
30   Saw us alight.

I look and see it there, shrinking, shrinking,
    I look back at it amid the rain
For the very last time; for my sand is sinking,
    And I shall traverse old love's domain
35   Never again.
THOMAS HARDY

A.11 Love

Love bade me welcome: yet my soul drew back,
    Guilty of dust and sin.
But quick-ey'd Love, observing me grow slack
    From my first entrance in,
5 Drew nearer to me, sweetly questioning,
    If I lack'd any thing.

A guest, I answer'd, worthy to be here:
    Love said, you shall be he.
I the unkind, ungrateful? Ah my dear,
10   I cannot look on thee.
Love took my hand, and smiling did reply,
    Who made the eyes but I?

Truth Lord, but I have marr'd them: let my shame
  Go where it doth deserve.
15 And know you not, says Love, who bore the blame?
  My dear, then I will serve.
You must sit down, says Love, and taste my meat:
  So I did sit and eat.

GEORGE HERBERT

A.12 The Sea and the Skylark

On ear and ear two noises too old to end
  Trench—right, the tide that ramps against the shore;
  With a flood or a fall, low lull-off or all roar,
Frequenting there while moon shall wear and wend.

5 Left hand, off land, I hear the lark ascend,
  His rash-fresh re-winded new-skeinèd score
  In crisps of curl off wild winch whirl, and pour
And pelt music, till none's to spill nor spend.

How these two shame this shallow and frail town!
10   How ring right out our sordid turbid time,
Being pure! We, life's pride and cared-for crown,

  Have lost that cheer and charm of earth's past prime:
Our make and making break, are breaking, down
  To man's last dust, drain fast towards man's first slime.

GERARD MANLEY HOPKINS

A.13 With Rue My Heart is Laden

With rue my heart is laden
  For golden friends I had,
For many a rose-lipt maiden
  And many a lightfoot lad.

5 By brooks too broad for leaping
  The lightfoot boys are laid;
The rose-lipt girls are sleeping
  In fields where roses fade.

A. E. HOUSMAN

A.15 Piano

Softly, in the dusk, a woman is singing to me;
Taking me back down the vista of years, till I see
A child sitting under the piano, in the boom of the tingling strings
And pressing the small, poised feet of a mother who smiles as she
    sings.

5 In spite of myself, the insidious mastery of song
Betrays me back, till the heart of me weeps to belong
To the old Sunday evenings at home, with winter outside
And hymns in the cosy parlour, the tinkling piano our guide.

So now it is vain for the singer to burst into clamour
10 With the great black piano appassionato. The glamour
Of childish days is upon me, my manhood is cast
Down in the flood of remembrance, I weep like a child for the
    past.

                        D. H. LAWRENCE

A.16 Time To Go

The day they had to go
Was brilliant after rain. Persimmons glowed
In the garden behind the castle.
Upon its wall lizards immutably basked
5 Like vitrified remains
Of an archaic, molten summer. Bronze
Cherubs shook down the chestnuts
From trees over a jetty, where fishing nets
Were sunshine hung out in skeins
10 To dry, and the fishing boats in their little harbour
Lay breathing asleep. Far
And free, the sun was writing, rewriting ceaselessly
Hieroglyphs on the lake—
Copying a million, million times one sacred

15 Vanishing word, peace.
    The globed hours bloomed. It was grape-harvest season

    And time to go. They turned and hurried away
    With never a look behind,
    As if they were sure perfection could only stay
20 Perfect now in the mind.
    And a backward glance would tarnish or quite devalue
    That innocent, golden scene.
    Though their hearts shrank, as if not till now they knew
    It was paradise where they had been,
25 They broke from the circle of bliss, the sunlit haven.
    Was it for guilt they fled?
    From enchantment? Or was it simply that they were driven
    By the migrant's punctual need?
    All these, but more—the demand felicity makes
30 For release from its own charmed sphere,
    To be carried into the world of flaws and heartaches,
    Reborn, though mortally, there.

    So, then, they went, cherishing their brief vision.
    One watcher smiled to see
35 Them go, and sheathed a flaming sword, his mission
    A pure formality.

C. DAY LEWIS

A.17 To The Public

Why hold that poets are so sensitive?
A thickskinned grasping lot who filch and eavesdrop,
Who enjoy ourselves at other men's expense,
Who, legislators or not, ourselves are lawless,
5 We do not need your indulgence, much less your pity;
With fewer qualms, we have rather more common sense
Than your Common Man, also of course more freedom,
With our burglars' and gunmen's fingers, our green fingers.
So, crude though we are, we get to times and places
10 And, saving your presence or absence, will continue
Throwing our dreams and guts in people's faces.

LOUIS MACNEICE

A.18 Lines in Praise of Tommy Atkins

Success to Tommy Atkins, he's a very brave man,
And to deny it there's few people can;
And to face his foreign foes he's never afraid,
Therefore he's not a beggar, as Rudyard Kipling has said.

5 No, he's paid by our Government, and is worthy of his hire,
And from our shores in time of war he makes our foes retire;
He doesn't need to beg; no, nothing so low;
No, he considers it more honourable to face a foreign foe.

No, he's not a beggar, he's a more useful man,
10 And, as Shakespeare has said, his life's but a span;
And at the cannon's mouth he seeks for reputation,
He doesn't go from door to door seeking a donation.

Oh, think of Tommy Atkins when from home far away,
Lying on the battlefield, earth's cold clay;
15 And a stone or his knapsack pillowing his head,
And his comrades lying near by him wounded and dead.

And while lying there, poor fellow, he thinks of his wife at home,
And his heart bleeds at the thought, and he does moan;
And down his cheek flows many a silent tear,
20 When he thinks of his friends and children dear.

Kind Christians, think of him when far, far away,
Fighting for his Queen and Country without dismay;
May God protect him wherever he goes,
And give him strength to conquer his foes.

25 To call a soldier a beggar is a very degrading name,
And in my opinion it's a very great shame;
And the man that calls him a beggar is not the soldier's friend,
And no sensible soldier should on him depend.

A soldier is a man that ought to be respected,
30 And by his country shouldn't be neglected;
For he fights our foreign foes, and in danger of his life,
Leaving behind him his relatives and his dear wife.

Then hurrah for Tommy Atkins, he's the people's friend,
Because when foreign foes assail us he does us defend;
35 He is not a beggar, as Rudyard Kipling has said,
No, he doesn't need to beg, he lives by his trade.

And in conclusion I will say,
Don't forget his wife and children when he's far away;
But try and help them all you can,
40 For remember Tommy Atkins is a very useful man.

WILLIAM MCGONAGALL

A.19 Asleep

Under his helmet, up against his pack,
After the many days of work and waking,
Sleep took him by the brow and laid him back.
And in the happy no-time of his sleeping,
5 Death took him by the heart. There was a quaking
Of the aborted life within him leaping . . .
Then chest and sleepy arms once more fell slack.
And soon the slow, stray blood came creeping
From the intrusive lead, like ants on track.

10 Whether his deeper sleep lie shaded by the shaking
Of great wings, and the thoughts that hung the stars,
High-pillowed on calm pillows of God's making
Above these clouds, these rains, these sleets of lead,
And these winds' scimitars;
15 —Or whether yet his thin and sodden head
Confuses more and more with the low mould,
His hair being one with the grey grass
And finished fields of autumn that are old . . .
Who knows? Who hopes? Who troubles? Let it pass!
20 He sleeps. He sleeps less tremulous, less cold
Than we who must awake, and waking, say Alas!

WILFRED OWEN

A.20 Belinda's Toilet

And now, unveil'd, the toilet stands display'd,
Each silver vase in mystic order laid.
First, robed in white, the nymph intent adores,
With head uncover'd, the cosmetic powers.
5 A heav'nly image in the glass appears,
To that she bends, to that her eye she rears;
Th' inferior priestess, at her altar's side,
Trembling, begins the sacred rites of pride.
Unnumber'd treasures ope at once, and here
10 The various offerings of the world appear;
From each she nicely culls with curious toil,
And decks the goddess with the glittering spoil.
This casket India's glowing gems unlocks,
And all Arabia breathes from yonder box.
15 The tortoise here and elephant unite,
Transform'd to combs, the speckled and the white.
Here files of pins extend their shining rows,
Puffs, powders, patches, Bibles, billet-doux.
Now awful beauty puts on all its arms;
20 The fair each moment rises in her charms,
Repairs her smiles, awakens every grace,
And calls forth all the wonders of her face;
Sees by degrees a purer blush arise,
And keener lightnings quicken in her eyes.
25 The busy sylphs surround their darling care,
These set the head, and those divide the hair,
Some fold the sleeve, while others plait the gown;
And Betty's praised for labours not her own.

ALEXANDER POPE
(from *The Rape of the Lock*)

A.21 Does it Matter?

Does it matter?—losing your legs? . . .
For people will always be kind,
And you need not show that you mind
When the others come in after hunting
5 To gobble their muffins and eggs.

Does it matter?—losing your sight? . . .
There's such splendid work for the blind;
And people will always be kind,
As you sit on the terrace remembering
10 And turning your face to the light.

Do they matter?—those dreams from the pit? . . .
You can drink and forget and be glad,
And people won't say that you're mad;
For they'll know that you've fought for your country
15 And no one will worry a bit.

Siegfried Sassoon

A.22 Sonnet 73

That time of year thou may'st in me behold
When yellow leaves, or none, or few, do hang
Upon those boughs which shake against the cold—
Bare ruin'd choirs, where late the sweet birds sang.
5 In me thou see'st the twilight of such day,
As after sunset fadeth in the west;
Which by and by black night doth take away,
Death's second self, that seals up all in rest.
In me thou see'st the glowing of such fire,
10 That on the ashes of his youth doth lie,
As the death-bed whereon it must expire,
Consum'd with that which it was nourish'd by.
This thou perceiv'st, which makes thy love more strong,
To love that well, which thou must leave ere long.

William Shakespeare

A.23 Carentan O Carentan

Trees in the old days used to stand
And shape a shady lane
Where lovers wandered hand in hand
Who came from Carentan.

5 This was the shining green canal
Where we came two by two
Walking at combat-interval.
Such trees we never knew.

The day was early June, the ground
10 Was soft and bright with dew.
Far away the guns did sound,
But here the sky was blue.

The sky was blue, but there a smoke
Hung still above the sea
15 Where the ships together spoke
To towns we could not see.

Could you have seen us through a glass
You would have said a walk
Of farmers out to turn the grass,
20 Each with his own hay-fork.

The watchers in their leopard suits
Waited till it was time,
And aimed between the belt and boot
And let the barrel climb.

25 I must lie down at once, there is
A hammer at my knee.
And call it death or cowardice,
Don't count again on me.

Everything's all right, Mother,
30 Everyone gets the same
At one time or another.
It's all in the game.

I never strolled, nor ever shall,
Down such a leafy lane.
35 I never drank in a canal,
Nor ever shall again.

There is a whistling in the leaves
And it is not the wind,
The twigs are falling from the knives
40 That cut men to the ground.

Tell me, Master-Sergeant,
The way to turn and shoot.
But the Sergeant's silent
That taught me how to do it.

45 O Captain, show us quickly
Our place upon the map.
But the Captain's sickly
And taking a long nap.

Lieutenant, what's my duty,
50 My place in the platoon?
He too's a sleeping beauty,
Charmed by that strange tune.

Carentan O Carentan
Before we met with you
55 We never yet had lost a man
Or known what death could do.

LOUIS SIMPSON

150

A.24 The Pylons

The secret of these hills was stone, and cottages
Of that stone made,
And crumbling roads
That turned on sudden hidden villages.

5 Now over these small hills, they have built the concrete
That trails black wire;
Pylons, those pillars
Bare like nude giant girls that have no secret.

The valley with its gilt and evening look
10 And the green chestnut
Of customary root,
Are mocked dry like the parched bed of a brook.

But far above and far as sight endures
Like whips of anger
15 With lightning's danger
There runs the quick perspective of the future.

This dwarfs our emerald country by its trek
So tall with prophecy:
Dreaming of cities
20 Where often clouds shall lean their swan-white neck.

STEPHEN SPENDER

A.25 Dark House

Dark house, by which once more I stand
    Here in the long unlovely street,
    Doors, where my heart was used to beat
So quickly, waiting for a hand,

5 A hand that can be clasp'd no more—
    Behold me, for I cannot sleep,
    And like a guilty thing I creep
At earliest morning to the door.

He is not here; but far away
10   The noise of life begins again,
    And ghastly thro' the drizzling rain
On the bald street breaks the blank day.
LORD TENNYSON (from In Memoriam)

A.26 A Blackbird Singing

It seems wrong that out of this bird,
Black, bold, a suggestion of dark
Places about it, there yet should come
Such rich music, as though the notes'
5 Ore were changed to a rare metal
At one touch of that bright bill.

You have heard it often, alone at your desk
In a green April, your mind drawn
Away from its work by sweet disturbance
10 Of the mild evening outside your room.

A slow singer, but loading each phrase
With history's overtones, love, joy
And grief learned by his dark tribe
In other orchards and passed on
15 Instinctively as they are now,
But fresh always with new tears.
R. S. THOMAS

A.27 Man

Weighing the steadfastness and state
    Of some mean things which here below reside,
Where birds like watchful clocks the noiseless date
    And intercourse of times divide,
5 Where bees at night get home and hive, and flowers,
        Early as well as late,
Rise with the sun and set in the same bowers;

I would, said I, my God would give
    The staidness of these things to man! for these
10 To his divine appointments ever cleave,
    And no new business breaks their peace;
The birds nor sow nor reap, yet sup and dine,
        The flowers without clothes live,
Yet Solomon was never drest so fine.

15 Man hath still either toys or care;
    He hath no root, nor to one place is tied,
But ever restless and irregular
    About the earth doth run and hide,
He knows he hath a home, but scarce knows where;
20   He says it is so far
That he hath quite forgot how to get there.

He knocks at all doors, strays and roams;
    Nay hath not so much wit as some stones have
Which in the darkest nights point to their homes,
25   By some hid sense their Maker gave;
Man is the shuttle to whose winding quest
        And passage through these looms
God ordered motion, but ordained no rest.

HENRY VAUGHAN

A.28 Sonnet

Surprised by joy—impatient as the Wind
I turned to share the transport—Oh! with whom
But Thee, deep buried in the silent tomb,
That spot which no vicissitude can find?
5 Love, faithful love, recalled thee to my mind—
But how could I forget thee? Through what power,
Even for the least division of an hour,
Have I been so beguiled as to be blind
To my most grievous loss?—That thought's return
10 Was the worst pang that sorrow ever bore,
Save one, one only, when I stood forlorn,
Knowing my heart's best treasure was no more;
That neither present time, nor years unborn
Could to my sight that heavenly face restore.

WILLIAM WORDSWORTH

A.29 When You Are Old and Grey

When you are old and grey and full of sleep,
And nodding by the fire, take down this book,
And slowly read, and dream of the soft look
Your eyes had once, and of their shadows deep;

5 How many loved your moments of glad grace,
And loved your beauty with love false or true,
But one man loved the pilgrim soul in you,
And loved the sorrows of your changing face;

And bending down beside the glowing bars,
10 Murmur, a little sadly, how Love fled
And paced upon the mountains overhead
And hid his face amid a crowd of stars.

W. B. YEATS

B MORE DIFFICULT POEMS

B.1 Lullaby
Lay your sleeping head, my love,
Human on my faithless arm;
Time and fevers burn away
Individual beauty from
5 Thoughtful children, and the grave
Proves the child ephemeral:
But in my arms till break of day
Let the living creature lie,
Mortal, guilty, but to me
10 The entirely beautiful.

Soul and body have no bounds:
To lovers as they lie upon
Her tolerant enchanted slope
In their ordinary swoon,
15 Grave the vision Venus sends
Of supernatural sympathy,
Universal love and hope;
While an abstract insight wakes
Among the glaciers and the rocks
20 The hermit's carnal ecstasy.

Certainty, fidelity
On the stroke of midnight pass
Like vibrations of a bell,
And fashionable madmen raise
25 Their pedantic boring cry:
Every farthing of the cost,
All the dreaded cards foretell,
Shall be paid, but from this night
Not a whisper, not a thought,
30 Not a kiss nor look be lost.

Beauty, midnight, vision dies:
Let the winds of dawn that blow
Softly round your dreaming head
Such a day of welcome show
35 Eye and knocking heart may bless,
Find our mortal world enough;
Noons of dryness find you fed
By the involuntary powers,
Nights of insult let you pass
40 Watched by every human love.

W. H. AUDEN

B. 2 Abel

My brother Cain, the wounded, liked to sit
Brushing my shoulder, by the staring water
Of life, or death, in cinemas half-lit
By scenes of peace that always turned to slaughter.

5 He liked to talk to me. His eager voice
Whispered the puzzle of his bleeding thirst,
Or prayed me not to make my final choice,
Unless we had a chat about it first.

And then he chose the final pain for me.
10 I do not blame his nature: he's my brother;
Nor what you call the times: our love was free,
Would be the same at any time; but rather

The ageless ambiguity of things
Which makes our life mean death, our love be hate.
15 My blood that streams across the bedroom sings:
'I am my brother opening the gate!'

DEMETRIOS CAPETANAKIS

B.3 The Song of The Mad Prince

Who said, 'Peacock Pie'?
The old King to the sparrow:
Who said, 'Crops are ripe'?
Rust to the harrow:
5 Who said, 'Where sleeps she now?
Where rests she now her head,
Bathed in eve's loveliness?'?—
That's what I said.

Who said, 'Ay, mum's the word'?
10 Sexton to willow:
Who said, 'Green dusk for dreams,
Moss for a pillow'?
Who said, 'All Time's delight
Hath she for narrow bed;
15 Life's troubled bubble broken'?—
That's what I said.

WALTER DE LA MARE

B.4 Explanation

When the pillars of smoke, that towered between heaven and
    earth
On the day we died, have thinned in the wind and drifted
And the hooded crow flaps home across the volcanic sky,
Somewhere beyond and below the littered horizon
5 (Out of the cave into the cold air)
Man, I suppose, will emerge and grow wise and read
What we have written in guilt, again with an innocent eye.

Then, if the desperate song we sang like storm-cocks
At the first flash, survives the ultimate thunder
10 To be dreamily misunderstood by the children of quieter men,
Remember that we who lived in the creeping shadow
(Dark over woodland, cloud and water)
Looked upon beauty often as though for the last time
And loved all things the more, that might never be seen again;

15 Who chewed the leaf, uncertain of seeing the hawthorn
Scatter its stars the length of a lane in summer,
Or fingered the sparrow's egg that might never be born a bird;
And wondered, even, whether the windflaw moving
Silently over the water's surface
20 Should gain the distant edge of the lake in safety
Before the inferno struck, whose echoes shall never be heard.

I sing to a child unborn, begotten in guilt
By us who have made the world unfit for his coming.
Our only comfort: that Christ was born in the cold.
25 I know, I know that a legion of singers before us
Looked their last on much that was lovely
And perished as we must perish. But who will remember
That most of them wept and died only because they were old?

PAUL DEHN

B.5 Zimri

In the first rank of these did Zimri stand:
A man so various, that he seemed to be
Not one, but all mankind's epitome:
Stiff in opinions, always in the wrong;
5 Was everything by starts, and nothing long;
But, in the course of one revolving moon,
Was chemist, fiddler, statesman, and buffoon;
Then all for women, painting, rhyming, drinking,
Besides ten thousand freaks that died in thinking.
10 Blest madman, who could every hour employ
With something new to wish, or to enjoy!
Railing and praising were his usual themes,
And both, to show his judgment, in extremes:
So over violent, or over civil,
15 That every man, with him, was God or Devil.
In squandering wealth was his peculiar art;
Nothing went unrewarded but desert.
Beggared by fools, whom still he found too late:
He had his jest, and they had his estate.
20 He laughed himself from Court; then sought relief
By forming parties, but could ne'er be chief:
For, spite of him, the weight of business fell
On Absalom and wise Achitophel:
Thus wicked but in will, of means bereft,
25 He left not faction, but of that was left.

JOHN DRYDEN
(from *Absalom and Achitophel*)

B.6 Rhapsody on a Windy Night

Twelve o'clock.
Along the reaches of the street
Held in a lunar synthesis,
Whispering lunar incantations
5 Dissolve the floors of memory
And all its clear relations,
Its divisions and precisions.
Every street-lamp that I pass
Beats like a fatalistic drum,
10 And through the spaces of the dark
Midnight shakes the memory
As a madman shakes a dead geranium.

Half-past one,
The street-lamp sputtered,
15 The street-lamp muttered,
The street-lamp said, 'Regard that woman
Who hesitates towards you in the light of the door
Which opens on her like a grin.
You see the border of her dress
20 Is torn and stained with sand,
And you see the corner of her eye
Twists like a crooked pin.'

The memory throws up high and dry
A crowd of twisted things;
25 A twisted branch upon the beach
Eaten smooth, and polished
As if the world gave up
The secret of its skeleton,
Stiff and white.
30 A broken spring in a factory yard,
Rust that clings to the form that the strength has left
Hard and curled and ready to snap.

            Half-past two,
        The street-lamp said,
35 'Remark the cat which flattens itself in the gutter,
        Slips out its tongue
        And devours a morsel of rancid butter.'
        So the hand of the child, automatic,
        Slipped out and pocketed a toy that was running along the quay,
40 I could see nothing behind that child's eye.
        I have seen eyes in the street
        Trying to peer through lighted shutters,
        And a crab one afternoon in a pool,
        An old crab with barnacles on his back,
45 Gripped the end of a stick which I held him.

            Half-past three,
        The lamp sputtered,
        The lamp muttered in the dark.
        The lamp hummed:
50 'Regard the moon,
        La lune ne garde aucune rancune,
        She winks a feeble eye,
        She smiles into corners.
        She smooths the hair of the grass.
55 The moon has lost her memory.
        A washed-out smallpox cracks her face,
        Her hand twists a paper rose,
        That smells of dust and eau de Cologne,
        She is alone
60 With all the old nocturnal smells
        That cross and cross across her brain.'
        The reminiscence comes
        Of sunless dry geraniums
        And dust in crevices,
65 Smells of chestnuts in the streets,
        And female smells in shuttered rooms,
        And cigarettes in corridors
        And cocktail smells in bars.

The lamp said,
70 'Four o'clock,
Here is the number on the door.
Memory!
You have the key,
The little lamp spreads a ring on the stair.
75 Mount.
The bed is open; the tooth-brush hangs on the wall,
Put your shoes at the door, sleep, prepare for life.'

The last twist of the knife.

T. S. ELIOT

B.7 Neutral Tones

We stood by a pond that winter day,
And the sun was white, as though chidden of God,
And a few leaves lay on the starving sod;
   —They had fallen from an ash, and were gray.

5 Your eyes on me were as eyes that rove
Over tedious riddles of years ago;
And words played between us to and fro—
   On which lost the more by our love.

The smile on your mouth was the deadest thing
10 Alive enough to have strength to die;
And a grin of bitterness swept thereby
   Like an ominous bird a-wing. . . .

Since then, keen lessons that love deceives,
And wrings with wrong, have shaped to me
15 Your face, and the God-curst sun, and a tree,
   And a pond edged with grayish leaves.

THOMAS HARDY

B.8 Now In My Hall

Now in my hall the rebel troopers stable
    Horses, whose iron hooves clang on the floor;
    They have hacked up to burn the great oak table,
    The wooden vine-leaves carved around the door;

5 And through my broken roof the waters beat,
    Beat, and the quick weather of sorrow falls,
    The rain coming down and mixed with withering sleet,
    Blurring the portraits and the storied walls.

And this cold wind and these black clouds that pelter
10   Have overtaken us both in the dark wood,
    Were blowing up already in childhood,

And they have driven me back to that bare hall
    My heart—I have no other place at all;
    But you were wiser, going elsewhere for shelter.
                                    JOHN HEATH-STUBBS

B.9 The Windhover

   To Christ our Lord

I caught this morning morning's minion, king-
    dom of daylight's dauphin, dapple-dawn-drawn Falcon, in his
    riding
Of the rolling level underneath him steady air, and striding
High there, how he rung upon the rein of a wimpling wing
In his ecstasy! then off, off forth on swing,
5   As a skate's heel sweeps smooth on a bow-bend: the hurl and
    gliding
Rebuffed the big wind. My heart in hiding
Stirred for a bird,—the achieve of, the mastery of the thing!

Brute beauty and valour and act, oh, air, pride, plume here
    Buckle! AND the fire that breaks from thee then, a billion
10 Times told lovelier, more dangerous, O my chevalier!

    No wonder of it: sheer plod makes plough down sillion
Shine, and blue-bleak embers, ah my dear,
    Fall, gall themselves, and gash gold-vermilion.
                                    G. M. HOPKINS

B.10 Tell Me Not Here

Tell me not here, it needs not saying,
    What tune the enchantress plays
In aftermaths of soft September
    Or under blanching mays,
5 For she and I were long acquainted
    And I knew all her ways.

On russet floors, by waters idle,
    The pine lets fall its cone;
The cuckoo shouts all day at nothing
10   In leafy dells alone;
And traveller's joy beguiles in autumn
    Hearts that have lost their own.

On acres of the seeded grasses
    The changing burnish heaves;
15 Or marshalled under moons of harvest
    Stand still all night the sheaves;
Or beeches strip in storms for winter
    And stain the wind with leaves.

Possess, as I possessed a season,
20   The countries I resign,
Where over elmy plains the highway
    Would mount the hills and shine,
And full of shade the pillared forest
    Would murmur and be mine.

25 For nature, heartless, witless nature,
    Will neither care nor know
What stranger's feet may find the meadow
    And trespass there and go,
Nor ask amid the dews of morning
30   If they are mine or no.

                A. E. HOUSMAN

B.11 A Woman Unconscious

Russia and America circle each other;
Threats nudge an act that were without doubt
A melting of the mould in the mother,
Stones melting about the root.

5 The quick of the earth burned out:
The toil of all our ages a loss
With leaf and insect. Yet flitting thought
(Not to be thought ridiculous)

Shies from the world-cancelling black
10 Of its playing shadow: it has learned
That there's no trusting (trusting to luck)
Dates when the world's due to be burned;

That the future's no calamitous change
But a malingering of now,
15 Histories, towns, faces that no
Malice or accident much derange.

And though bomb be matched against bomb,
Though all mankind wince out and nothing endure—
Earth gone in an instant flare—
20 Did a lesser death come

Onto the white hospital bed
Where one, numb beyond her last of sense,
Closed her eyes on the world's evidence
And into pillows sunk her head?

TED HUGHES

B.12 To Paint a Water Lily

A green level of lily leaves
Roofs the pond's chamber and paves

The flies' furious arena: study
These, the two minds of this lady.

5 First observe the air's dragonfly
That eats meat, that bullets by

Or stands in space to take aim;
Others as dangerous comb the hum

Under the trees. There are battle-shouts
10 And death-cries everywhere hereabouts

But inaudible, so the eyes praise
To see the colours of these flies

Rainbow their arcs, spark, or settle
Cooling like beads of molten metal

15 Through the spectrum. Think what worse
Is the pond-bed's matter of course;

Prehistoric bedragonned times
Crawl that darkness with Latin names,

Have evolved no improvements there,
20 Jaws for heads, the set stare,

Ignorant of age as of hour –
Now paint the long-necked lily-flower

Which, deep in both worlds, can be still
As a painting, trembling hardly at all

25 Though the dragonfly alight,
Whatever horror nudge her root.

TED HUGHES

B.13 Ode on a Grecian Urn

Thou still unravished bride of quietness,
   Thou foster-child of silence and slow time,
Sylvan historian, who canst thus express
   A flowery tale more sweetly than our rhyme:
5 What leaf-fringed legend haunts about thy shape
   Of deities or mortals, or of both,
     In Tempe or the dales of Arcady?
What men or gods are these? What maidens loth?
   What mad pursuit? What struggle to escape?
10   What pipes and timbrels? What wild ecstasy?

Heard melodies are sweet, but those unheard
   Are sweeter; therefore, ye soft pipes, play on;
Not to the sensual ear, but, more endeared,
   Pipe to the spirit ditties of no tone:
15 Fair youth, beneath the trees, thou canst not leave
   Thy song, nor ever can those trees be bare;
     Bold Lover, never, never canst thou kiss,
Though winning near the goal—yet, do not grieve;
   She cannot fade, though thou hast not thy bliss,
20   For ever wilt thou love, and she be fair!

Ah, happy, happy, boughs! that cannot shed
   Your leaves, nor ever bid the Spring adieu;
And, happy melodist, unwearied,
   For ever piping songs for ever new;
25 More happy love! more happy, happy love!
   For ever warm and still to be enjoyed,
     For ever panting, and for ever young;
All breathing human passion far above,
   That leaves a heart high-sorrowful and cloyed,
30   A burning forehead, and a parching tongue.

Who are these coming to the sacrifice?
    To what green altar, O mysterious priest,
Lead'st thou that heifer lowing at the skies,
    And all her silken flanks with garlands dressed?
35 What little town by river or sea shore,
    Or mountain-built with peaceful citadel,
      Is emptied of its folk, this pious morn?
And, little town, thy streets for evermore
    Will silent be; and not a soul to tell
40   Why thou art desolate, can e'er return.

O Attic shape! Fair attitude! with brede
    Of marble men and maidens overwrought,
With forest branches and the trodden weed;
    Thou, silent form, dost tease us out of thought
45 As doth eternity: Cold Pastoral!
    When old age shall this generation waste,
      Thou shalt remain, in midst of other woe
Than ours, a friend to man, to whom thou say'st,
    'Beauty is truth, truth beauty,'—that is all
50   Ye know on earth, and all ye need to know.

JOHN KEATS

B.14 Wreath Makers in Leeds Marketplace

A cocksure boy in the gloom of the gilded market bends
With blunt fingers a bow of death, and the flowers work with him.
They fashion a grave of grass with dead bracken and fine ferns.

An old woman with a mouthful of wires and a clutch of irises
5 Mourns in perpetual black, and her fists with the sunken rings
Rummage in the fragrant workbasket of a wreath.

A laughing Flora dangles a cross between her thighs
Like a heavy child, feeds it with pale plump lilies, crimson
Roses, wraps it in greenery and whips it with wires.

10 And here a grieving flower god with a lyre in his arms
Fumbles mute strings in the rough-gentle machine of his fingers,
His eyes wet violets, and in his mouth a last carnation . . .

Mourners all, they know not why they mourn,
But work and breathe the perfumes of their trade
15 (Those flower-vines, through which death more keenly speaks)

With suitable dispassion; though they know their emblems fade,
And they at last must bear a yellowed wreath
That other hands, and other harvesters have made.

JAMES KIRKUP

B.15 Here

Swerving east, from rich industrial shadows
And traffic all night north; swerving through fields
Too thin and thistled to be called meadows,
And now and then a harsh-named halt, that shields
5 Workmen at dawn; swerving to solitude
Of skies and scarecrows, haystacks, hares and pheasants,
And the widening river's slow presence,
The piled gold clouds, the shining gull-marked mud,

Gathers to the surprise of a large town:
10 Here domes and statues, spires and cranes cluster
Beside grain-scattered streets, barge-crowded water,
And residents from raw estates, brought down
The dead straight miles by stealing flat-faced trolleys,
Push through plate-glass swing doors to their desires—
15 Cheap suits, red kitchen-ware, sharp shoes, iced lollies,
Electric mixers, toasters, washers, driers—

A cut-price crowd, urban yet simple, dwelling
Where only salesmen and relations come
Within a terminate and fishy-smelling
20 Pastoral of ships up streets, the slave museum,
Tattoo-shops, consulates, grim head-scarfed wives;
And out beyond its mortgaged half-built edges
Fast-shadowed wheat-fields, running high as hedges,
Isolate villages, where removed lives

25 Loneliness clarifies. Here silence stands
   Like heat. Here leaves unnoticed thicken,
   Hidden weeds flower, neglected waters quicken,
   Luminously-peopled air ascends;
   And past the poppies bluish neutral distance
30 Ends the land suddenly beyond a beach
   Of shapes and shingle. Here is unfenced existence:
   Facing the sun, untalkative, out of reach.

PHILIP LARKIN

B.16 Lines on a Young Lady's Photograph Album

At last you yielded up the album, which,
Once open, sent me distracted. All your ages
Matt and glossy on the thick black pages!
Too much confectionery, too rich:
5 I choke on such nutritious images.

My swivel eye hungers from pose to pose—
In pigtails, clutching a reluctant cat;
Or furred yourself, a sweet girl-graduate;
Or lifting a heavy-headed rose
10 Beneath a trellis, or in a trilby hat

(Faintly disturbing, that, in several ways)—
From every side you strike at my control,
Not least through these disquieting chaps who loll
At ease about your earlier days:
15 Not quite your class, I'd say, dear, on the whole.

But o, photography! as no art is,
Faithful and disappointing! that records
Dull days as dull, and hold-it smiles as frauds
And will not censor blemishes
20 Like washing-lines, and Hall's Distemper boards,

But shows the cat as disinclined, and shades
A chin as doubled when it is, what grace
Your candour thus confers upon her face!
How overwhelmingly persuades
25 That this is a real girl in a real place,

In every sense empirically true!
Or is it just *the past*? Those flowers, that gate,
These misty parks and motors, lacerate
Simply by being over; you
30 Contract my heart by looking out of date.

Yes, true; but in the end, surely, we cry
Not only at exclusion, but because
It leaves us free to cry. We know *what was*
Won't call on us to justify
35 Our grief, however hard we yowl across

The gap from eye to page. So I am left
To mourn (without a chance of consequence)
You, balanced on a bike against a fence;
To wonder if you'd spot the theft
40 Of this one of you bathing; to condense,

In short, a past that no one can now share,
No matter whose your future; calm and dry,
It holds you like a heaven, and you lie
Unvariably lovely there,
45 Smaller and clearer as the years go by.
                              PHILIP LARKIN

B.17 Slow Movement

Waking, he found himself in a train, andante,
With wafers of early sunlight blessing the unknown fields
And yesterday cancelled out, except for yesterday's papers
    Huddling under the seat.

5 It is still very early, this is a slow movement;
The viola-player's hand like a fish in a glass tank
Rises, remains quivering, darts away
    To nibble invisible weeds.

Great white nebulae lurch against the window
10 To deploy across the valley, the children are not yet up
To wave us on—we pass without spectators,
    Braiding a voiceless creed.

And the girl opposite, name unknown, is still
Asleep and the colour of her eyes unknown
15 Which might be wells of sun or moons of wish
    But it is still very early.

The movement ends, the train has come to a stop
In buttercup fields, the fiddles are silent, the whole
Shoal of silver tessellates the aquarium
20   Floor, not a bubble rises . . .

And what happens next on the programme we do not know,
If, the red line topped on the gauge, the fish will go mad in the tank
Accelerando con forza, the sleeper open her eyes
    And, so doing, open ours.

LOUIS MACNEICE

B.18 Soap Suds

This brand of soap has the same smell as once in the big
House he visited when he was eight: the walls of the bathroom
                                            open
To reveal a lawn where a great yellow ball rolls back through a
                                            hoop
To rest at the head of a mallet held in the hands of a child.

5 And these were the joys of that house: a tower with a telescope;
Two great faded globes, one of the earth, one of the stars;
A stuffed black dog in the hall; a walled garden with bees;
A rabbit warren; a rockery; a vine under glass; the sea.

To which he has now returned. The day of course is fine
10 And a grown-up voice cries Play! The mallet slowly swings,
Then crack, a great gong booms from the dog-dark hall and the
                                            ball
Skims forward through the hoop and then through the next and
                                            then

Through hoops where no hoops were and each dissolves in turn
And the grass has grown head-high and an angry voice cries Play!
15 But the ball is lost and the mallet slipped long since from the
                                            hands
Under the running tap that are not the hands of a child.

LOUIS MACNEICE

B.19 The Thousand Things

Dry vine leaves burn in an angle of the wall.
Dry vine leaves and a sheet of paper, overhung
by the green vine.
From an open grate in an angle of the wall
5 dry vine leaves and dead flies send smoke up
into the green vine where grape clusters go
ignored by lizards. Dry vine leaves
and a few dead flies on fire
and a Spanish toffee spat
10 into an angle of the wall
make a smell that calls to mind
the thousand things. Dead flies go,
paper curls and flares,
Spanish toffee sizzles and the smell
15 has soon gone over the wall.

A naked child jumps over the threshold,
waving a green spray of leaves of vine.

CHRISTOPHER MIDDLETON

B.20 Redeployment

They say the war is over. But water still
Comes bloody from the taps, and my pet cat
In his disorder vomits worms which crawl
Swiftly away. Maybe they leave the house.
5 These worms are white, and flecked with the cat's blood.

The war may be over. I know a man
Who keeps a pleasant souvenir, he keeps
A soldier's dead blue eyeballs that he found
Somewhere—hard as chalk, and blue as slate.
10 He clicks them in his pocket while he talks.

And now there are cockroaches in the house,
They get slightly drunk on DDT,
Are fast, hard, shifty—can be drowned but not
Without you hold them under quite some time.
15 People say the Mexican kind can fly.

The end of the war. I took it quietly
Enough. I tried to wash the dirt out of
My hair and from under my fingernails,
I dressed in clean white clothes and went to bed.
20 I heard the dust falling between the walls.

HOWARD NEMEROV

B.21 Futility

Move him into the sun—
Gently its touch awoke him once,
At home, whispering of fields unsown.
Always it woke him, even in France,
5 Until this morning and this snow.
If anything might rouse him now
The kind old sun will know.

Think how it wakes the seeds,—
Woke, once, the clays of a cold star.
10 Are limbs, so dear-achieved, are sides,
Full-nerved—still warm—too hard to stir?
Was it for this the clay grew tall?
—O what made fatuous sunbeams toil
To break earth's sleep at all?

WILFRED OWEN

B.22 A Portrait of Lord Hervey

Yet let me flap this bug with gilded wings,
This painted child of dirt, that stinks and stings;
Whose buzz the witty and the fair annoys,
Yet wit ne'er tastes, and beauty ne'er enjoys:
5 So well-bred spaniels civilly delight
In mumbling of the game they dare not bite.
Eternal smiles his emptiness betray,
As shallow streams run dimpling all the way.
Whether in florid impotence he speaks,
10 And, as the prompter breathes, the puppet squeaks;
Or at the ear of Eve, familiar toad!
Half froth, half venom, spits himself abroad,
In puns, or politics, or tales, or lies,
Or spite, or smut, or rhymes, or blasphemies.
15 His wit all see-saw, between that and this,
Now high, now low, now master up, now miss,
And he himself one vile antithesis.
Amphibious thing! that acting either part,
The trifling head, or the corrupted heart,
20 Fop at the toilet, flatterer at the board,
Now trips a lady, and now struts a lord.
Eve's tempter thus the Rabbins have expressed,
A cherub's face, a reptile all the rest;
Beauty that shocks you, parts that none will trust;
25 Wit that can creep, and pride that licks the dust.

ALEXANDER POPE
(from *Epistle to Dr Arbuthnot*)

B.23 Annotations of Auschwitz

I

When the burnt flesh is finally at rest,
The fires in the asylum grates will come up
And wicks turn down to darkness in the madman's eyes.

II

My suit is hairy, my carpet smells of death,
5 My toothbrush handle grows a cuticle.
I have six million foulnesses of breath.
Am I mad? The doctor holds my testicles
While the room fills with the zyklon B I cough.

III

On Piccadilly underground I fall asleep—
10 I shuffle with the naked to the steel door,
Now I am only ten from the front—I wake up—
We are past Gloucester Rd., I am not a Jew,
But scratches web the ceiling of the train.

IV

Around staring buildings the pale flowers grow;
15 The frenetic butterfly, the bee made free by work,
Rouse and rape the pollen pads, the nectar stoops.
The rusting railway ends here. The blind end in Europe's gut.
Touch one piece of unstrung barbed wire—
Let it taste blood: let one man scream in pain,
20 Death's Botanical Gardens can flower again.

V

A man eating his dressing in the hospital
Is lied to by his stomach. It's a final feast to him
Of beef, blood pudding and black bread.
The orderly can't bear to see this mimic face
25 With its prim accusing picture after death.

On the stiff square a thousand bodies
Dig up useless ground—he hates them all,
These lives ignoble as ungoverned glands.
They fatten in statistics everywhere
30 And with their sick, unkillable fear of death
They crowd out peace from executioners' sleep.

VI

Forty thousand bald men drowning in a stream—
The like of light on all those bobbing skulls
Has never been seen before. Such death, says the painter,
35 Is worthwhile—it makes a colour never known.
It makes a sight that's unimagined, says the poet.
It's nothing to do with me, says the man who hates
The poet and the painter. Six million deaths can hardly
Occur at once. What do they make? Perhaps
40 An idiot's normalcy. I need never feel afraid
When I salt the puny snail—cruelty's grown up
And waits for time and men to bring into its hands
The snail's adagio and all the taunting life
Which has not cared about or guessed its tortured scope.

VII

45 London is full of chickens on electric spits,
    Cooking in windows where the public pass.
  This, say the chickens, is their Auschwitz,
    And all poultry eaters are psychopaths.

PETER PORTER

B.24 In my Craft or Sullen Art

In my craft or sullen art
Exercised in the still night
When only the moon rages
And the lovers lie abed
5 With all their griefs in their arms,
I labour by singing light
Not for ambition or bread
Or the strut and trade of charms
On the ivory stages
10 But for the common wages
Of their most secret heart.

Not for the proud man apart
From the raging moon I write
On these spindrift pages
15 Nor for the towering dead
With their nightingales and psalms
But for the lovers, their arms
Round the griefs of the ages,
Who pay no praise or wages
20 Nor heed my craft or art.

DYLAN THOMAS

B.25 It Rains

It rains, and nothing stirs within the fence
Anywhere through the orchard's untrodden, dense
Forest of parsley. The great diamonds
Of rain on the grassblades there is none to break,
5 Or the fallen petals further down to shake.

And I am nearly as happy as possible,
To search the wilderness in vain though well,
To think of two walking, kissing there,
Drenched, yet forgetting the kisses of the rain:
10 Sad, too, to think that never, never again,

Unless alone, so happy shall I walk
In the rain. When I turn away, on its fine stalk
Twilight has fined to naught, the parsley flower
Figures, suspended still and ghostly white,
15 The past hovering as it revisits the light.

EDWARD THOMAS

B.26 Here

I am a man now.
Pass your hand over my brow,
You can feel the place where the brains grow.

I am like a tree,
5   From my top boughs I can see
The footprints that led up to me.

There is blood in my veins
That has run clear of the stain
Contracted in so many loins.

10 Why, then, are my hands red
With the blood of so many dead?
Is this where I was misled?

Why are my hands this way
That they will not do as I say?
15 Does no God hear when I pray?

I have nowhere to go.
The swift satellites show
The clock of my whole being is slow.

It is too late to start
20 For destinations not of the heart.
I must stay here with my hurt.

                                    R. S. Thomas

B.27 An Old Man

Looking upon this tree with its quaint pretension
Of holding the earth, a leveret, in its claws,
Or marking the texture of its living bark,
A grey sea wrinkled by the winds of years,
5 I understand whence this man's body comes,
Its veins and fibres, the bare boughs of bone,
The trellised thicket, where the heart, that robin,
Greets with a song the seasons of the blood.

But where in meadow or mountain shall I match
10 The individual accent of the speech
That is the ear's familiar? To what sun attribute
The honeyed warmness of his smile?
To which of the deciduous brood is german
The angel peeping from the latticed eye?

R. S. Thomas

B.28 The Wild Swans at Coole

The trees are in their autumn beauty,
The woodland paths are dry,
Under the October twilight the water
Mirrors a still sky;
5 Upon the brimming water among the stones
Are nine-and-fifty swans.

The nineteenth autumn has come upon me
Since I first made my count;
I saw, before I had well finished,
10 All suddenly mount
And scatter wheeling in great broken rings
Upon their clamorous wings.

I have looked upon those brilliant creatures,
And now my heart is sore.
15 All's changed since I, hearing at twilight,
The first time on this shore,
The bell-beat of their wings above my head,
Trod with a lighter tread.

Unwearied still, lover by lover,
20 They paddle in the cold
Companionable streams or climb the air;
Their hearts have not grown old;
Passion or conquest, wander where they will,
Attend upon them still.

25 But now they drift on the still water,
Mysterious, beautiful;
Among what rushes will they build,
By what lake's edge or pool
Delight men's eyes when I awake some day
30 To find they have flown away?

W. B. YEATS

C POEMS FOR COMPARISON

C.1 Drummer Hodge

They throw in Drummer Hodge, to rest
  Uncoffined—just as found:
His landmark is a kopje-crest
  That breaks the veldt around;
5 And foreign constellations west
  Each night above his mound.

Young Hodge the Drummer never knew—
  Fresh from his Wessex home—
The meaning of the broad Karoo,
10   The Bush, the dusty loam,
And why uprose to nightly view
  Strange stars amid the gloam.

Yet portion of that unknown plain
  Will Hodge for ever be;
15 His homely Northern breast and brain
  Grow to some Southern tree,
And strange-eyed constellations reign
  His stars eternally.

The Soldier

If I should die, think only this of me:
  That there's some corner of a foreign field
That is for ever England. There shall be
  In that rich earth a richer dust conceal'd;
5 A dust whom England bore, shaped, made aware,
  Gave, once, her flowers to love, her ways to roam,
A body of England's, breathing English air,
  Wash'd by the rivers, blest by suns of home,

  And think, this heart, all evil shed away,
10 A pulse in the eternal mind, no less
    Gives somewhere back the thoughts by England given;
  Her sights and sounds; dreams happy as her day;
  And laughter, learnt of friends; and gentleness,
    In hearts at peace, under an English heaven.

C.2 Scaffolding

Masons, when they start upon a building,
Are careful to test out the scaffolding;

Make sure that the planks won't slip at busy points,
Secure all ladders, tighten bolted joints.

5 And yet all this comes down when the job's done
Showing off walls of sure and solid stone.

So if, my dear, there sometimes seem to be
Old bridges breaking between you and me

Never fear. We may let the scaffolds fall
10 Confident that we have built our wall.

The Silken Tent

She is as in a field a silken tent
At midday when a sunny summer breeze
Has dried the dew and all its ropes relent,
So that in guys it gently sways at ease,
5 And its supporting central cedar pole,
That is its pinnacle to heavenward
And signifies the sureness of the soul,
Seems to owe naught to any single cord,
But strictly held by none, is loosely bound
10 By countless silken ties of love and thought
To everything on earth the compass round,
And only by one's going slightly taut
In the capriciousness of summer air
Is of the slightest bondage made aware.

C.3 The End of the World

Quite unexpectedly as Vasserot
The armless ambidextrian was lighting
A match between his great and second toe
And Ralph the lion was engaged in biting
5 The neck of Madame Sossman while the drum
Pointed, and Teeny was about to cough
In waltz-time swinging Jocko by the thumb—
Quite unexpectedly the top blew off:

And there, there overhead, there, there, hung over
10 Those thousands of white faces, those dazed eyes,
There in the starless dark, the poise, the hover,
There with vast wings across the cancelled skies,
There in the sudden blackness the black pall
Of nothing, nothing, nothing—nothing at all.

End of the World

The world's end came as a small dot
    at the end of a sentence. Everyone died
without ado, and nobody cried
    enough to show the measure of it.

5 God said: 'I do not love you', quite
    quietly, but with a final note;
it seemed the words caught in his throat,
    or else he stifled a yawn as the trite

    phrase escaped his dust-enlivening lips.
10   At least, there was no argument,
no softening tact, no lover's cant,
    but sudden vacuum, total eclipse

of sense and meaning. The world had gone
    and everything on it, except the lives
15 all of us had to live: the wives,
    children, clocks which ticked on,

unpaid bills, enormous power-blocks
    chock-full of arms demanding peace,
and the prayerful in a state of grace
20   pouncing on bread and wine like hawks.

C.4 Arms and the Boy

Let the boy try along this bayonet-blade
How cold steel is, and keen with hunger of blood;
Blue with all malice, like a madman's flash;
And thinly drawn with famishing for flesh.

5 Lend him to stroke these blind, blunt bullet-heads
Which long to nuzzle in the hearts of lads,
Or give him cartridges of fine zinc teeth,
Sharp with the sharpness of grief and death.

For his teeth seem for laughing round an apple.
10 There lurk no claws behind his fingers supple;
And God will grow no talons at his heels,
Nor antlers through the thickness of his curls.

The Kiss

To these I turn, in these I trust—
Brother Lead and Sister Steel.
To his blind power I make appeal,
I guard her beauty clean from rust.

5 He spins and burns and loves the air,
And splits a skull to win my praise;
But up the nobly marching days
She glitters naked, cold and fair.

Sweet Sister, grant your soldier this:
10 That in good fury he may feel
The body where he sets his heel
Quail from your downward darting kiss.

C.5 Hawk Roosting

I sit in the top of the wood, my eyes closed.
Inaction, no falsifying dream
Between my hooked head and hooked feet:
Or in sleep rehearse perfect kills and eat.

5 The convenience of the high trees!
The air's buoyancy and the sun's ray
Are of advantage to me;
And the earth's face upward for my inspection.

My feet are locked upon the rough bark.
10 It took the whole of Creation
To produce my foot, my each feather:
Now I hold Creation in my foot

Or fly up, and revolve it all slowly—
I kill where I please because it is all mine.
15 There is no sophistry in my body:
My manners are tearing off heads—

The allotment of death.
For the one path of my flight is direct
Through the bones of the living.
20 No arguments assert my right:

The sun is behind me.
Nothing has changed since I began.
My eye has permitted no change.
I am going to keep things like this.

Tamer and Hawk

I thought I was so tough,
But gentled at your hands
Cannot be quick enough
To fly for you and show
5 That when I go I go
At your commands.

Even in flight above
I am no longer free:
You seeled me with your love,
10 I am blind to other birds—
The habit of your words
Has hooded me.

As formerly, I wheel
I hover and I twist,
15 But only want the feel
In my possessive thought,
Of catcher and of caught
Upon your wrist.

You but half-civilize,
20 Taming me in this way.
Through having only eyes
For you I fear to lose,
I lose to keep, and choose
Tamer as prey.

C.6 Employment

If, as a flower doth spread and die,
Thou wouldst extend me to some good,
Before I were by frost's extremity
Nipped in the bud;

5   The sweetness and the praise were Thine,
But the extension and the room
Which in Thy garland I should fill were mine
At Thy great doom.

For as Thou dost impart Thy grace,
10   The greater shall our glory be;
The measure of our joys is in this place,
The stuff with Thee.

Let me not languish, then, and spend
A life as barren to Thy praise
15 As is the dust to which that life doth tend,
But with delays.

All things are busy; only I
Neither bring honey with the bees,
Nor flowers to make that, nor the husbandry
20   To water these.

I am no link of Thy great chain,
But all my company is a weed.
Lord, place me in Thy consort; give one strain
To my poor reed.

Thou Art Indeed Just, Lord

Thou art indeed just, Lord, if I contend
With thee; but, sir, so what I plead is just.
Why do sinners' ways prosper? and why must
Disappointment all I endeavour end?
5   Wert thou my enemy, O thou my friend,
How wouldst thou worse, I wonder, than thou dost
Defeat, thwart me? Oh, the sots and thralls of lust
Do in spare hours more thrive than I that spend,
Sir, life upon thy cause. See, banks and brakes
10 Now, leavèd how thick! lacèd they are again
With fretty chervil, look, and fresh wind shakes
Them; birds build—but not I build; no, but strain,
Time's eunuch, and not breed one work that wakes.
Mine, O thou lord of life, send my roots rain.

C.7 And death shall have no dominion

And death shall have no dominion.
Dead men naked they shall be one
With the man in the wind and the west moon;
When their bones are picked clean and the clean bones gone,
5   They shall have stars at elbow and foot;
Though they go mad they shall be sane,
Though they sink through the sea they shall rise again;
Though lovers be lost love shall not;
And death shall have no dominion.

10 And death shall have no dominion.
Under the windings of the sea
They lying long shall not die windily;
Twisting on racks when sinews give way,
Strapped to a wheel, yet they shall not break;
15 Faith in their hands shall snap in two,
And the unicorn evils run them through;
Split all ends up they shan't crack;
And death shall have no dominion.

And death shall have no dominion.
20 No more may gulls cry at their ears
Or waves break loud on the seashores;
Where blew a flower may a flower no more
Lift its head to the blows of the rain;
Though they be mad and dead as nails,
25 Heads of the characters hammer through daisies;
Break in the sun till the sun breaks down,
And death shall have no dominion.

Death be not proud
Death, be not proud, though some have callèd thee
Mighty and dreadful, for thou art not so:
For those whom thou think'st thou dost overthrow
Die not, poor Death; nor yet canst thou kill me.
5 From Rest and Sleep, which but thy pictures be,
Much pleasure, then from thee much more must flow;
And soonest our best men with thee do go—
Rest of their bones and souls' delivery!
Thou'rt slave to Fate, Chance, kings, and desperate men,
10 And dost with poison, war, and sickness dwell;
And poppy or charms can make us sleep as well
And better than thy stroke; why swell'st thou then?
    One short sleep past, we wake eternally,
    And Death shall be no more: Death, thou shalt die!

D POEMS WITH QUESTIONS

D.1 Hymn to Diana

      Queen and huntress, chaste and fair,
         Now the sun is laid to sleep,
     Seated in thy silver chair,
         State in wonted manner keep:
5   Hesperus entreats thy light,
         Goddess excellently bright.

     Earth, let not thy envious shade
         Dare itself to interpose;
     Cynthia's shining orb was made
10   Heaven to clear when day did close:
         Bless us then with wishèd sight,
         Goddess excellently bright.

     Lay thy bow of pearl apart,
         And thy crystal-shining quiver;
15 Give unto the flying hart
         Space to breathe, how short soever:
         Thou that mak'st a day of night,
         Goddess excellently bright.

It was the lovely moon

It was the lovely moon—she lifted
Slowly her white brow among
Bronze cloud-waves that ebbed and drifted
Faintly, faintlier afar.
5 Calm she looked, yet pale with wonder,
Sweet in unwonted thoughtfulness,
Watching the earth that dwindled under
Faintly, faintlier afar.
It was the lovely moon that lovelike
10 Hovered over the wondering, tired
Earth, her bosom grey and dovelike,
Hovering beautiful as a dove. . . .
The lovely moon: her soft light falling
Lightly on roof and poplar and pine—
15 Tree to tree whispering and calling,
Wonderful in the silvery shine
Of the round, lovely, thoughtful moon.

1 What is the attitude of each poet towards his subject?
2 Contrast the two poems from the point of view of verse form, rhyme scheme, and diction.
3 To what extent does the imagery of the second poem contribute to the overall effect?
4 Which is the more successful poem?

D.2 To Some Builders of Cities

You have thrust Nature out, to make
A wilderness where nothing grows
But forest of unbudding stone
(The sparrow's lonely for his boughs);
5 You fling up citadels to stay
The soft invasion of the rose.

But though you put the earth in thrall
And ransack all her fragrant dowers,
Her old accomplice, Heaven, will plot
10 To take with stars your roofs and towers;
And neither stone nor steel can foil
That ambuscade of midnight flowers.

London

See what a mass of gems the city wears
Upon her broad live bosom! row on row
Rubies and emeralds and amethysts glow.
See! that huge circle, like a necklace, stares
5 With thousands of bold eyes to heaven, and dares
The golden stars to dim the lamps below
And in the mirror of the mire I know
The moon has left her image unawares.
That's the great town at night: I see her breasts,
10 Prick'd out with lamps they stand like huge black towers,
I think they move! I hear her panting breath.
And that's her head where the tiara rests.
And in her brain, through lanes as dark as death,
Men creep like thoughts. . . . The lamps are like pale flowers.

1 What is the attitude of each poet towards the city?
2 Comment on the appropriateness of the imagery.
3 What are the strengths and weaknesses of the two poems?

D.3 Go, lovely rose

Go, lovely rose—
Tell her that wastes her time and me,
  That now she knows,
When I resemble her to thee
5   How sweet and fair she seems to be.

  Tell her that's young,
And shuns to have her graces spied,
  That hadst thou sprung
In deserts where no men abide,
10   Thou must have uncommended died

  Small is the worth
Of beauty from the light retired:
  Bid her come forth,
Suffer herself to be desired,
15   And not blush so to be admired.

  Then die, that she
The common fate of all things rare
  May read in thee;
How small a part of time they share,
20   That are so wondrous sweet and fair.

Now sleeps the crimson petal

Now sleeps the crimson petal, now the white;
Nor waves the cypress in the palace walk;
Nor winks the gold fin in the porphyry font:
The firefly wakens: waken thou with me.

5   Now droops the milk-white peacock like a ghost,
And like a ghost she glimmers on to me.

Now lies the Earth all Danae to the stars,
And all thy heart lies open unto me.

Now slides the silent meteor on, and leaves
10 A shining furrow, as thy thoughts in me.

Now folds the lily all her sweetness up,
And slips into the bosom of the lake:
So fold thyself, my dearest, thou, and slip
Into my bosom and be lost in me.

1 Both of these poems were intended to be set to music. What
  features of these poems might have led you to this conclusion?
2 Compare the ways in which the poets use natural description
  in the poems.
3 Although both these poems could be classed as love poems, how
  do they differ in terms of tone and feeling?

D.4 Walter Llywarch

I am, as you know, Walter Llywarch,
Born in Wales of approved parents,
Well goitred, round in the bum;
Sure prey of the slow virus
5 Bred in quarries of grey rain.

Born in autumn at the right time
For hearing stories from the cracked lips
Of old folk dreaming of summer,
I piled them on to the bare hearth
10 Of my own fancy to make a blaze
To warm myself, but achieved only
The smoke's acid that brings the smart
Of false tears into the eyes.

Months of fog, months of drizzle:
15 Thought wrapped in the grey cocoon
Of race, of place, awaiting the sun's
Coming; but when the sun came
Striking the hills with a hot hand,
Wings were spread only to fly
20 Round and round in a cramped cage,
Or beat in vain at the sky's window.

School in the week; on Sunday chapel:
Tales of a land fairer than this
Were not so tall, for others had proved it
25 Without the grave's passport; they sent
Its fruit home for ourselves to taste . . .

Walter Llywarch! The words were the name
On a lost letter that never came
For one who waited in the long queue
30 Of life that wound through a Welsh valley.
I took instead, as others had done
Before, a wife from the back pew
In chapel, rather to share the rain

Of winter evenings than to intrude
35 On her pale body. And yet we lay
For warmth together and laughed to hear
Each new child's cry of despair.

Evening Voluntary
No sound is uttered,—but a deep
And solemn harmony pervades
The hollow vale from steep to steep,
And penetrates the glades.
5 Far-distant images draw nigh,
Called forth by wondrous potency
Of beamy radiance, that imbues
Whate'er it strikes with gem-like hues!
In vision exquisitely clear,
10 Herds range along the mountain side;
And glistening antlers are descried;
And gilded flocks appear.
Thine is the tranquil hour, purpureal Eve!
But long as god-like wish, or hope divine,
15 Informs my spirit, ne'er can I believe
That this magnificence is wholly thine!
—From worlds most quickened by the sun
A portion of the gift is won;
An intermingling of Heaven's pomp is spread
20 On ground which British shepherds tread!

1 These two poems are concerned with describing a particular
landscape and the feelings it evokes in the poet. Comment on the
differences between the two, taking into account both emotion
and description.
2 How effective are these passages from the point of view of the
style the poet has chosen to use?
3 Both these poems deal with heaven and religion in general. What
different attitudes are revealed in each one?

D.5 Inversnaid

This darksome burn, horseback brown,
His rollrock highroad roaring down,
In coop and in comb the fleece of his foam
Flutes and low to the lake falls home.

5 A windpuff-bonnet of fawn-froth
Turns and twindles over the broth
Of a pool so pitchblack, fell-frowning,
It rounds and rounds Despair to drowning.

Degged with dew, dappled with dew
10 Are the groins of the braes that the brook treads through,
Wiry heathpacks, flitches of fern,
And the beadbonny ash that sits over the burn.

What would the world be, once bereft
Of wet and wildness? Let them be left,
15 O let them be left, wildness and wet;
Long live the weeds and the wilderness yet.

1 Choose three phrases that seem unconventional or unusual and explain them carefully in your own words.
2 Apart from using phrases which require some analysis and explanation, what other aspects of the poet's style seem out of the ordinary?
3 To what extent is the poet justified in using a style like this? Can it be said to create fresh insights in the reader, or is it merely playing with words?

D.6 The Capital

Quarter of pleasures where the rich are always waiting,
Waiting expensively for miracles to happen,
Dim-lighted restaurant where lovers eat each other,
Cafe where exiles have established a malicious village:

5 You with your charm and your apparatus have abolished
The strictness of winter and the spring's compulsion;
Far from your lights the outraged punitive father,
The dullness of mere obedience here is apparent.

So with orchestras and glances, soon you betray us
10 To belief in our infinite powers; and the innocent
Unobservant offender falls in a moment
Victim to his heart's invisible furies.

In unlighted streets you hide away the appalling;
Factories where lives are made for temporary use
15 Like collars or chairs, rooms where the lonely are battered
Slowly like pebbles into fortuitous shapes.

But the sky you illumine, your glow is visible far
Into the dark countryside, the enormous, the frozen,
Where, hinting at the forbidden like a wicked uncle,
20 Night after night to the farmer's children you beckon.

1 Explain the following passages:

(a) where the lonely are battered . . . into fortuitous shapes
(b) the outraged punitive father
(c) heart's invisible furies
(d) factories where lives are made for temporary use.

2 Explain in your own words what the poet thinks are the attractions of the capital.

3 Describe in detail the style of the poem and show how suitable it is to the effect the poet is trying to create.

D.7 First Meeting with a Possible Mother-in-law

She thought, without the benefit of knowing,
You, who had been hers, were not any more.
We had locked our love in to leave nothing showing
From the room her handiwork had crammed before;
5 But—much revealing in its figured sewing—
A piece of stuff hung out, caught in the door.
I caused the same suspicion I watched growing:
Who could not tell what whole the part stood for?

There was small likeness between her and me:
10 Two strangers left upon a bare top landing,
I for a prudent while, she totally.

But, eyes turned from the bright material hint,
Each shared too long a second's understanding,
Learning the other's terms of banishment.

1 What do we learn of the attitude of the mother to her possible son-in-law?
2 Examine the imagery of the poem.
3 Discuss the part played by rhyme and rhythm.
4 How successful is the poem in its attempt to convey the relationships between the people concerned?

D.8 The Men Who Wear My Clothes

Sleepless I lay last night and watched the slow
Procession of the men who wear my clothes:
First, the grey man with bloodshot eyes and sly
Gestures miming what he loves and loathes.

5 Next came the cheery knocker-back of pints,
The beery joker, never far from tears
Whose loud and public vanity acquaints
The careful watcher with his private fears.

And then I saw the neat-mouthed gentle man
10 Defer politely, listen to the lies,
Smile at the tedious talk and gaze upon
The little mirrors in the speaker's eyes.

The men who wear my clothes walked past my bed
And all of them looked tired and rather old;
15 I felt a chip of ice melt in my blood.
Naked I lay last night and very cold.

Write an appreciation of this poem.

Glossary of Technical Terms

ABSTRACT Ideas, emotions or concepts which cannot be apprehended by the senses. See also CONCRETE.

ACCENT The overall pattern of stressed syllables in a passage of verse. See also METRE.

ALEXANDRINE See METRE.

ALLEGORY A difficult term to define in that it usually means talking about abstract ideas in terms of people, places or events. Bunyan, in his allegorical novel *Pilgrim's Progress*, describes his spiritual life in terms of a journey with many pitfalls and dangers. Each detail in the book represents part of his religious life; for example, Pilgrim's imprisonment in Doubting Castle symbolises Bunyan's own temporary disillusion with his faith. Another well-known example of the allegorical novel is George Orwell's *Animal Farm*. One of the most famous examples of allegory in verse is Chaucer's *Roman de la Rose*, where the poet describes falling in love in terms of entering a garden and picking a rose. See also SYMBOL.

ALLITERATION The repetition of consonants in a line of poetry or in closely adjacent lines:

'Full *f*athom *f*ive thy *f*ather lies,
Of his bones are coral made:'
(Shakespeare)

See also ASSONANCE.

ALLITERATIVE VERSE Anglo-Saxon verse depended on alliteration as the basis of its metrical shape, and this tradition continued for a long time side by side with rhyming and syllable-counting metres and verse forms. William Langland was still using this type of verse in the middle of the fourteenth century:

'In a somer seson Whan soft was the sonne,
I shope me in shroudes As I a shepe were.'

AMPHIBRAIC METRE See METRE.

ANALYSIS A considered attempt to write or talk about the characteristics and qualities of a piece of verse.

ANAPAESTIC METRE See METRE.

ANTI-CLIMAX An attempt to produce humour by a sudden change from the sublime to the ridiculous;

> 'And thou, Great Anna, Whom three Realms obey,
> Dost sometime counsel take, and Sometime Tea;'
>
> (Pope)

When the effect is unintentional it is called Bathos. See also CLIMAX.

ARCHAISM Using an out-of-date style of speech, form of words or syntax in poetry. Coleridge uses many archaisms in his poem *The Ancient Mariner*:

> "Hold off! unhand me, grey-beard loon!'
> Eftsoons his hand dropped he.'

ASSONANCE The repetition of a vowel-sound in the same line or closely adjacent lines of poetry:

> 'Life like a dome of many-coloured glass,
> Stains the white radiance of eternity;'
>
> (Shelley)

See also ALLITERATION.

AUGUSTAN A term used to describe a period when eminent works of literature were written. Initially it was applied to the reign of the Emperor Augustus (27 B.C.–A.D. 14) because Virgil, Horace and Ovid were flourishing at this time. In English literature the Augustan period was from c. 1660–1780 when the most important writers, Dryden, Pope and Swift, were strongly influenced by classical ideas.

BALLAD Originally a dance, but it has come to mean a narrative poem written in four-line stanzas, rhyming *abcb* or *abab*; sometimes there is also a refrain. (See page 70.)

BATHOS See ANTI-CLIMAX.

BLANK VERSE Verse which does not rhyme, usually written in iambic pentameters. It has proved the most widely used form of poetry in many different periods; Shakespeare used it in his plays, Milton in *Paradise Lost* and Wordsworth in most of his poems. See also METRE.

BUCOLIC Dealing with herdsmen and shepherds. See also PASTORAL.

BURLESQUE An imitation of either a serious literary composition or the ideas of a group of people with the purpose of making them look ridiculous; one of the most famous poetic burlesques is Samuel Butler's *Hudibras* where the author makes fun of religious hypocrisy. See also PARODY.

CAESURA The brief pause in the middle of a line of poetry:

> 'Fix'd were their habits; they arose betimes,
> Then pray'd their hour, and sang their party rhymes.'
>
> (Crabbe)

CANTO Originally a song, but the term has come to mean the major divisions of a long narrative poem; Byron's *Don Juan*, for example, is divided into cantos.

CAROLINE A term describing the authors of the reign of Charles I; these include Herbert, Herrick, Crashaw, Vaughan and Carew who were famous for their religious and love poetry; and the CAVALIER poets, Suckling and Lovelace who wrote love songs, and poems about the Civil Wars.

CAVALIER See CAROLINE.

CHAUCERIAN Connected with the life or work of Chaucer; it is also used to describe a group of Scottish poets of the fourteenth century, including Henryson and Dunbar, who were influenced by Chaucer.

CLASSICAL (*a*) Poetry or literature in general that is accepted as setting the highest standards.

(*b*) The ideas and methods of the famous Latin and Greek authors.

(*c*) The poetry of the seventeenth and eighteenth century (see AUGUSTAN) which was influenced by Latin and Greek art. This is sometimes referred to as Neo-Classical poetry.

CLICHÉ A phrase which has ceased to have much meaning because it has been used so much: 'the winds of change', 'the man in the street' are two modern examples.

CLIMAX The most convincing part of an argument or series of ideas; the part of a poem where the emotional pressure is the greatest.

CONCEIT A particularly startling image such as was very popular with the Metaphysical poets. Dr. Johnson, who had little sympathy with this school of writers, described the conceit as 'the witty yoking of opposites'.

> 'Only a sweet and virtuous soul,
> Like seasoned timber never gives;
> But though the whole world turn to coal,
> Then chiefly lives.'
> (Herbert)

See also METAPHYSICAL; IMAGERY.

CONCRETE Tangible, dealing with objects that can be apprehended by the senses. See also ABSTRACT.

CONVENTION See TRADITION.

COUPLET Two consecutive lines of verse which rhyme and usually have the same metre:

> 'Had we but World enough and time,
> This coyness, lady, were no crime,'
> (Marvell)

CRITICISM The evaluation of a piece of literature—not necessarily finding fault with it.

'Criticism was meant a standard of judging well, the chiefest part of which is to observe those excellencies which should delight a reasonable reader.' (Dryden)

DACTYLIC METRE See METRE.

DICTION The choice of words a poet makes to create a particular effect or tone. See Chapter 2, Diction.

DIDACTIC A poem or piece of prose that is intended to teach the reader or to give him advice; one of the most famous examples of didactic poetry is Milton's *Paradise Lost* which was intended

'To justify the ways of God to man.'

DIMETER See METRE.

DIRGE A song to commemorate the death of a famous person; a burial song; a THRENODY. A dirge is usually a public song of lament; an ELEGY which is very similar, is a more personal and meditative type of DIRGE. Famous examples of this type of poem include Shelley's *Adonais*, Gray's *Elegy written in a Country Churchyard* and the song for Fidele in Shakespeare's *Cymbeline* (p. 33).

DISSONANCE Words which sound very harsh; sometimes it forms part of a poet's method as in Hopkins'

'No worst, there is none. Pitched past pitch of grief,
More pangs will, schooled at forepangs, wilder wring.'

DOUBLE RHYME See RHYME.

DRAFT The first, usually incomplete versions of a poem. See Chapter 4.

DRAMATIC MONOLOGUE A poem in which the speaker is not the author but a character from the poem. Many of Browning's most famous poems, such as *My Last Duchess*, are fine examples of this type of poem.

ECLOGUE A type of poem in the PASTORAL tradition; in Classical literature it is a dialogue between two shepherds, but modern poets have used the form more loosely, as a conversation poem between two people, e.g. MacNeice's *Eclogue from Iceland*.

ELEGY See DIRGE.

ELISION See METRE.

ELIZABETHAN A term which describes the literature of the reign of Queen Elizabeth (1558–1603). It is also loosely used of literature from the reign of James I (1603–1625) and sometimes even of Charles I (1625–1648).

ELLIPSIS Words that are necessary to the completion of a sentence from a grammatical point of view are sometimes omitted by writers, as in this example from *Macbeth*:

> 'What! all my pretty chickens and their dam
> At one fell swoop?'

ENJAMBEMENT See METRE.

EMBLEM See SYMBOL.

EPIC A long narrative poem which deals with matters of major importance, such as the destruction of Troy or the creation of the world. Sometimes called a HEROIC poem. Another important aspect of the epic is that God or gods are involved in the action, as in *Paradise Lost* by Milton, and Virgil's *Aeneid*.

EPIGRAM A very short poem ending in a witty turn of thought. This epigram was written by Pope for the collar of the Prince of Wales' dog:

> 'I am his Highness' dog at Kew;
> Pray tell me sir, whose dog are you?'

EPITAPH Verse written on a tomb to commemorate the person buried there.

EPITHALAMIUM A poem in praise of marriage. This type of verse is also called a PROTHALAMIUM by Spenser.

EUPHEMISM Using a more pleasant form of words to describe something ugly or distasteful: 'the dog was put to sleep'.

EYE-RHYME See RHYME.

FABLE A poem or story in which animals often take the place of humans; the purpose of the poem is usually to teach a moral or to make satirical comments on human society. Perhaps the most famous example is Aesop's *Fables*.

FEMININE ENDING See METRE.

FIGURATIVE LANGUAGE Language which is based on comparisons or word pictures; 'to stand the strain' originally was concerned with ropes, but now the phrase has a much wider meaning. See also IMAGE; METAPHOR; SYMBOL.

FOOT See METRE.

FORM The type of verse (e.g. sonnet, blank verse) which a poet thinks is most appropriate to what he wants to communicate; the shape of ideas and emotions in a poem. (See Chapter 2, Sounds, Rhymes and Forms.)

FREE VERSE Poetry which disregards the traditional disciplines of rhyme and metre, and relies on the nature of the content to create the form or shape of the poem.

GENRE (a) Type or style of verse used by the poets of a certain period. Up to the twentieth century it was possible to recognise the different *genres* of the Elizabethans, the Augustans, or the Romantics; today there is no single style that is accepted by all contemporary poets. (b) The term is also used to describe different forms of literature— short story, epic, one-act play, etc.

GEORGIAN POETRY Five anthologies of poems written early in this century by Brooke, Drinkwater, Munro, Gibson and others, and published between 1912 and 1922.

HAIKU A type of Japanese poem in a very small compass with seventeen syllables arranged in three lines of five, seven and five syllables:

> 'On the downward path,
> Again the sound of bird-song
> And the shining grass.'

In translation, these strict rules are frequently waived. (See p. 117.)

HEPTAMETER See METRE.

HEROIC COUPLET The Iambic pentameter couplet was sometimes called heroic because it was used in epic or heroic poetry. See also COUPLET; EPIC.

HEXAMETER See METRE.

HYPERBOLE Intentional exaggeration in order to emphasise a particular point:

> 'An hundred years should go to praise
> Thine eyes, and on thy forehead gaze.'
> (Marvell)

IAMBIC VERSE See METRE.

IDYLL A story, frequently in verse, of innocent people in ideal surroundings. Similar to the pastoral tradition in many ways, but it can deal with more heroic situations and events, as in Tennyson's *Idylls of the King*.

IMAGERY Comparisons between two or more usually unrelated objects or ideas to clarify the sense or add a different tone or feeling to the poetry:

> 'Sleep, that knits up the ravelled sleeve of care'
> (Shakespeare)

See also METAPHOR; SYMBOL; SIMILE.

INTERNAL RHYME See RHYME.

INVECTIVE Criticism of a personal kind, usually without reference to the rights and wrongs of the case. A bitter attack, as in Pope's *Dunciad*.

INVERTED FOOT See METRE.

IRONY A milder and less destructive type of sarcasm: saying the opposite of what is in fact meant. Originally it meant 'taking the arguments of another person as your own in order to point out the foolishness of his ideas'. In Dramatic Irony, a chance remark early in the play takes on great significance in that it foreshadows subsequent events of great importance.

LAMENT A poem or song of mourning. See DIRGE.

LAMPOON A scurrilous personal attack or caricature in verse, popular in the seventeenth and eighteenth century.

LATINISM A word or construction peculiar to Latin, used in another language:

> 'Far off from these a slow and silent stream,
> Lethe the river of oblivion rolls
> Her watery labyrinth,'
>
> (Milton)

LYRIC Originally a song sung to a lyre, but it has come to mean a short poem which expresses the poet's feelings and ideas; perhaps a poem that could easily be set to music, as many of Burns' love lyrics have been.

METAPHOR A comparison implied or stated between two usually unconnected objects:

> 'The sea that bares her bosom to the moon;'
> (Wordsworth)

See also IMAGERY; SIMILE; SYMBOL.

METAPHYSICAL (a) Philosophical, to do with the unseen or speculative.

        (b) The name given by Dryden to a group of poets writing c. 1590–1650; these included Donne, Herbert, Crashaw, Vaughan and many others. They were given the name because of their use of a particularly intellectual type of imagery even in love poems. In one of Donne's poems parted lovers are compared to the legs of a pair of compasses:

> 'If they be two, they are two so
> As stiff twin compasses are two,
> Thy soul the fixed foot, makes no show
> To move, but doth, if the other do.'

See also CONCEIT.

METRE In English poetry, metre is made up of recurring patterns of stressed and unstressed syllables. If we look closely at these two lines from Keats' poem,

> 'When I have fears that I may cease to be
> Before my pen hath gleaned my teeming brain',

we can see that each line has ten syllables, arranged in pairs—one unstressed syllable followed by a stressed. Each of these units of rhythm is called a Foot and this basic pattern is repeated five times, giving us five feet to a line:

'When I | have fears | that I | may cease | to be'

Using the symbols ᴗ and — to denote unstressed and stressed syllables respectively, we are able to split up the lines according to their metrical shape:

$$\text{'When } \overset{\cup}{\text{I}} \mid \overset{\cup}{\text{have}} \overset{\_}{\text{fears}} \mid \text{that } \overset{\_}{\text{I}} \mid \overset{\cup}{\text{may}} \overset{\_}{\text{cease}} \mid \overset{\cup}{\text{to}} \overset{\_}{\text{be}}$$

$$\overset{\cup}{\text{Before}} \mid \overset{\cup}{\text{my}} \overset{\_}{\text{pen}} \mid \text{hath } \overset{\_}{\text{gleaned}} \mid \overset{\cup}{\text{my}} \overset{\_}{\text{tee}}\text{ming } \overset{\cup}{\text{brain}}\text{'}.$$

This process of sorting out the metrical pattern of a poem is called Scansion.

A line of poetry with one foot is called a monometer

,,	,,	,,	,,	,,	two feet	,,	dimeter
,,	,,	,,	,,	,,	three ,,	,,	trimeter
,,	,,	,,	,,	,,	four ,,	,,	tetrameter
,,	,,	,,	,,	,,	five ,,	,,	pentameter
,,	,,	,,	,,	,,	six ,,	,,	hexameter
,,	,,	,,	,,	,,	seven ,,	,,	heptameter
,,	,,	,,	,,	,,	eight ,,	,,	octameter.

(A six foot iambic line is also called an Alexandrine.)

There are many different patterns of syllables which make up the various feet used in English poetry. The most usual is the Iambic foot—unstressed followed by stressed (ᴗ —):

'That time of year thou mayst in me behold
When yellow leaves, or none, or few do hang'
(Shakespeare)

<u>Trochaic foot</u>: stressed followed by unstressed (— ᴗ)

'Home art gone and ta'en thy wages.'

<u>Dactylic foot</u>: stressed followed by two unstressed (— ᴗ ᴗ)

'Half a league, half a league, half a league onwards.'

<u>Anapaestic foot</u>: two unstressed followed by stressed (ᴗ ᴗ —)

'When I went to the Bar as a very young man.'

Amphibraic foot: unstressed followed by stressed followed by unstressed (∪ — ∪)

> 'For sudden the worst turns the best to the brave.'

Spondaic foot: two stressed syllables (— —)

> 'A̅ll who̅m wa̅r, dea̅rth, a̅ge, a̅gŭe, ty̅rannĭe̅s,
> Despa̅ir, la̅w, cha̅nce ha̅th sla̅ine,'

End stopping occurs when the sense stops at the end of a line of poetry:

> 'O Mistress mine, where are you roaming?
> O stay and hear, your true love's coming,'

When the sense of the line carries over to the next line this is called
Enjambement:

> 'Sweetest love I do not go
> For weariness of thee,
> Nor in hope the world can show
> A fitter love for me.'

Elision is a device frequently used by poets; it involves omitting an
unstressed syllable so that the line conforms to the metrical pattern:

> 'Moving of the'earth brings harms and fears'

When a line has a Feminine Ending, there is an extra unstressed syllable
at the end of the line:

> '∪By bro̅oks | ∪too bro̅ad | ∪for le̅ap | ∪ing'

When there is an extra stressed syllable at the end of the line, this is
called a Masculine Ending:

> '—Ti̅ger, | —ti̅ger | burn̅ing | bri̅ght
> In the forests of the night.'

Inverted foot occurs when the metre of a particular foot is turned round.
Usually it is the first foot in a line that is treated in this way:

> 'And some | times like | a glean | er thou | dost keep
> Steady | thy lad | en head | across | a brook.'

MIDDLE ENGLISH The transitional language spoken in parts of England from
roughly 1100–1500. It was based on Anglo-Saxon and gradually
developed into modern English.

MOCK HEROIC Writing about trivialities but using a very high-flown style; one of the most famous examples of the mock-heroic is Pope's *The Rape of the Lock* where an unimportant quarrel is treated in a style more worthy of the *Iliad*. See also HEROIC COUPLET.

MONOMETER See METRE.

MOOD The mood of a poem could be described as the overall emotional effect or feeling of the poem; the impression that the reader is left with when he has read it carefully.

MOTIF A dominant theme which occurs from time to time in a poem, or in many other art forms.

MYTH Legend or story which frequently interprets natural forces in terms of gods or heroes. Poets have used many myths as the basis for their work; Shelley drew on the classical legend of Prometheus—the man who was punished by the gods for bringing the gift of fire to earth—in order to write his poem in praise of artistic freedom, *Prometheus Unbound*.

NARRATIVE VERSE Verse that tells a story; famous examples are *The Canterbury Tales* by Chaucer and Arnold's *Sohrab and Rustum*. Few poems are solely narrative, to the exclusion of other forms of subject matter such as description or emotion; most poems have some narrative basis, however slight it may be.

OCCASIONAL VERSE Poetry written for a special occasion; sometimes it is poetry that deals with topical issues. *On the Late Massacre in Piedmont* by Milton and *The Wreck of the Deutschland* by Hopkins are examples of occasional verse that is of a very high quality.

OCTAMETER See METRE.

ODE A verse form derived from Classical Literature which is very similar to the LYRIC in that both were meant to be sung; the difference between the two lies in the fact that the ode was usually intended to be performed before an audience, whereas the lyric was more personal. Keats' four great odes and Wordsworth's *Intimations of Immortality* are among the best known, but they differ radically from the classical patterns of Pindar and Horace.

ONOMATOPOEIA The use of words that echo their meaning in their sound, such as *splash*, *murmur*.

> 'The bare black cliff clang'd round him, as he based
> His feet on juts of slippery crag that rang
> Sharp-smitten with the dint of armed heels.'
> (Tennyson)

PANEGYRIC Praise of a person or institution; a formal speech.

PARADOX A statement which appears contradictory, but when considered, contains a great deal of truth.

> 'Cowards die many times before their death'
>
> (Shakespeare)

PARARHYME See RHYME.

PARODY An attempt to make fun of a particular author or style by closely copying his themes or methods. Lewis Carroll's poem which begins

> ' "You are old, Father William," the young man said,
> "And your hair has become very white,
> And yet you incessantly stand on your head—
> Do you think, at your age, it is right?" '

was a parody of Southey's poem *The Old Man's Comforts and how he gained them*. Whereas a burlesque is an attempt to ridicule particular ideas or methods of writing specifically in order to produce humour or satire, a parody is a more strictly literary exercise where the particular style is exactly copied, usually, but not always, for a humorous effect.

PASTORAL This is a poetic tradition which poets have used in many ages; the pastoral poem deals with the countryside, and more especially the life of shepherds, usually from an unrealistic point of view: the weather is always fine, and the shepherds do no work other than composing verses and songs. One of the finest expressions of the pastoral tradition is Marlowe's *The Passionate Shepherd to his Love*:

> 'The Shepheard's Swain shall dance and sing
> For thy delight each May-morning,
> If these delights thy mind may move;
> Then live with me and be my love.'

PATHETIC FALLACY Ruskin's phrase to describe the idea that inanimate objects have feelings and are able to sympathise with human situations.

> 'Where even the little brambles would not yield,
> But clutched and clung to them like sorrowing hands'
>
> (Owen)

PEDANTRY A great show of learning.

PERSONIFICATION Describing inanimate objects in terms of people and animals, as if the inanimate objects had minds or feelings.

> 'The yellow fog that rubs its back upon the window panes'
>
> (Eliot)

PLAGIARISM The deliberate taking of another work and using it as if it were your own.

PLATITUDE A trite or pointless statement made as though it were really important.

POETIC DICTION The type of language which is used by a poet to create his effects. It has involved different choices for different poets: to the Augustans it meant 'words refined from the grossness of domestic use'; to Wordsworth it meant 'the real language of men in a state of vivid sensation'.

QUATRAIN A stanza which is made up of four lines which may have various rhyme schemes; this is the commonest English stanza form.

QUINTAIN A stanza made up of five lines.

REALISM 'The art of bringing something close to us, making it palpable and vivid, by sharply observed or sharply imagined detail.' (C. S. Lewis)

RHETORIC An attempt to convince people by using heightened language, either spoken or written.

RHYME Complete Rhyme:

> 'The noisy geese that gabbled o'er the pool,
> The playful children just let loose from school'

By studying this quotation closely we can draw out the four factors necessary to make a perfect rhyme:

(a) Two identically pronounced consonants . . . poo*l*
school

(b) Two identically pronounced vowels . . . p*oo*l
sch*oo*l

(c) A difference in the previous consonant . . . *p*ool
sc*h*ool

(d) Identical stressing of the two rhyming words or parts of words.

It is not essential to make a rhyme by having vowel plus consonant; consonant followed by vowel is also acceptable.

Single Rhyme is rhyme made with one syllable, as in the above example.

Double Rhyme and Triple Rhyme are made up of two and three syllables respectively, e.g. duty/beauty, slenderly/tenderly.

Polysyllabic Rhyme is often used to produce a comic effect:

> 'My days of love are over;
> The charms of maid, wife, and still less of widow,
> Can make the fool of which they did before,
> In short I must not lead the life I did do;
> The credulous hope of mutual minds is o'er,
> The copious use of claret is forbid too.'   (Byron)

Incomplete Rhyme. Rhymes may appear incomplete or inaccurate in different ways; the vowels may not nowadays be pronounced in the same way, e.g. love/move, wind/mind. This latter type is sometimes referred to as an Eye Rhyme. Several poets have deliberately chosen to weaken the force of the rhyme by making either consonant or vowel different; this is usually called Half Rhyme, Slant Rhyme or Para-Rhyme:

> 'It seemed that out of battle I escaped
> Down some profound dull tunnel, long since scooped
> Through granites which titanic wars had groined.
> Yet also there encumbered sleepers groaned,'

> (Owen)

Internal Rhyme occurs where a rhyme is used in the middle as well as at the end of a line:

> 'We were the first that ever burst
> Into that silent sea.'
> (Coleridge)

RHYTHM See METRE and the relevant part of Chapter 2.

ROMANTICISM This is a term that is used to describe many different forms; painting, music as well as poetry. Broadly speaking, the Romantic poets, such as Coleridge, Wordsworth, Shelley, Keats and Byron, were in revolt against many of the ideas of the eighteenth century; in spite of widely contrasting views on poetry, the Romantics generally accepted most of the statements put forward by Wordsworth and Coleridge in the *Preface to the Lyrical Ballads*. These principles included:

(a) The natural goodness of man, and the validity of his own emotions.
(b) The importance of Nature in the correct development of man's aesthetic and moral sensibility.
(c) A desire to change society by removing many of the restrictions of Church and State.

SARCASM Basically a wounding or cutting remark. The two Greek words from which this term is derived mean 'tearing flesh'. The purpose behind the use of sarcasm is to cause pain, whether the criticism is justified or not.

SATIRE An attempt to ridicule the follies of men, institutions or ideas, often with the intention of correcting the defects that are being criticised. In the preface to *The Battle of the Books*, Swift wrote, 'Satire is a sort of glass wherein beholders do generally discover everybody's face but their own'. Famous examples of satire are Dryden's *Absalom and Achitophel* and Pope's *Dunciad*.

SCANSION The study of syllabic stress and metrical form. See also METRE.

SESTET A stanza form using six lines; the term is frequently applied to the last stanza of a Petrarchan sonnet. See also SONNET.

SIMILE A comparison for the purpose of explanation, allusion or decoration which uses 'like' or 'as':

> 'O, my love is like a red, red rose
> That's newly sprung in June'
>   (Burns)

See also IMAGERY; METAPHOR; SYMBOL.

SONNET The sonnet has developed from a very popular Italian verse form of the period of Petrarch and Michelangelo. It spread into France at the beginning of the sixteenth century where Ronsard and other poets used it to great effect; round about 1550 it was introduced into England by Wyatt and Surrey and quickly gained an immense popularity. The Elizabethans wrote many sonnet sequences which were loosely narrative in form, but it was also used as occasional verse; part of a gentleman's education was to be able to write a sonnet off the cuff.

The Petrarchan sonnet was divided into an octave and a sestet, making fourteen lines in all. The rhyme-scheme was based on two opening quatrains which rhymed abba, abba; and the sestet was made up of two tercets rhyming cdc, dcd; or, cde, cde, or, three pairs of lines cd, cd, cd.

In the Shakespearean sonnet the lines are grouped into three quatrains; abab, cdcd, efef, followed by a couplet, gg.

The Miltonic sonnet is a development of the Petrarchan form, the difference being that there is no pause between the octave and the sestet, and the latter usually rhymes cdcdcd.

SPONDAIC METRE See METRE.

STANZA Lines of verse which are grouped together to form a pattern which is repeated throughout the poem.

STRESS See METRE.

STRUCTURE The way in which the various ideas or emotions in a poem are arranged in an attempt to form a coherent and satisfying shape. Sometimes it can mean the metrical pattern.

STYLE The methods of writing adopted by a poet or group of poets. Many different aspects of poetry are grouped together in this term, choice of vocabulary and syntax, use of different types of figurative language, overall tone of the passage in question, etc.

SYMBOL A simple image or comparison which represents or sums up a much larger sphere of activity or interest; the cross has always been the symbol for Christianity—even such diverse aspects of Christianity as devotion and worship, theology and the historical basis of the religion.

SYMBOLISTS The name given to a group of French poets which included Mallarmé, Verlaine and Rimbaud; their idea was to represent concepts and emotions more clearly in the form of symbols. Several modern poets writing in English (e.g. Yeats, Dylan Thomas and T. S. Eliot) were influenced by the Symbolists.

TETRAMETER See METRE.

THRENODY See DIRGE.

TONE The prevailing feeling or attitude behind a poem; the overall impression of a piece of verse. Sometimes it refers more specifically to the moral outlook of the poem.

TRADITION A poetic tradition could be described as the peculiar style or choice of subject matter adopted by a school of poets, or even by poets from a particular country. Once a tradition is well established (such as writing sonnets or ballads) it can continue to have an effect on succeeding generations of poets.

TRIMETER See METRE.

TRIPLE RHYME See RHYME.

TROCHEE See METRE.

VERSE PARAGRAPH A group of lines, frequently in blank verse, which form a unit within themselves, without any overall stanza pattern. Several poets have used this form with great effectiveness, e.g. Milton in *Paradise Lost*.

VERS LIBRE See FREE VERSE.

VICTORIAN Literature from the period of Queen Victoria.

WIT Cleverness, facility with words. In different periods it has meant different things; to the seventeenth century it meant a comparison which 'compels interest by its far-fetched or outrageous quality'; to the eighteenth century, 'thoughts and words elegantly adapted to the subject'.

Key to Authors quoted Anonymously

Key to passages at end of Chapter 6

(a) Opening of Swinburne's *A Forsaken Garden*.

(b) From Pope's *Essay on Man*.

(c) By Ogden Nash.

(d) From Dickens' description of the death of Little Nell in his novel *The Old Curiosity Shop*. The passage is reproduced *verbatim*, though the lineation has, of course, been changed, and initial letters of words at the beginning of 'lines' have been made capitals.

(e) From the 'In Memoriam' column of an English evening newspaper.

(f) *Considering the Snail*, a poem by Thom Gunn. Does the knowledge that this piece was originally broken into verse lines alter your response to the question 'Is it poetry?' Should it?

How would *you* divide the given words into lines of verse? Be prepared to justify your decisions.

(g) By E. E. Cummings.

(h) From Chapter 45 of *The Mayor of Casterbridge*, by Thomas Hardy.

Authors of Poems Printed Anonymously in Part Two

Section C

C.1   Thomas Hardy, Rupert Brooke

C.2   Seamus Heaney, Robert Frost

C.3   Archibald MacLeish, Tony Connor

C.4   Wilfred Owen, Siegfried Sassoon

C.5   Ted Hughes, Thom Gunn

C.6   George Herbert, G. M. Hopkins

C.7   Dylan Thomas, John Donne

Section D

D.1   Ben Jonson, John Freeman

D.2   Stanley Snaith, Alfred Douglas

D.3   Edmund Waller, Alfred Tennyson

D.4   R. S. Thomas, William Wordsworth

D.5   G. M. Hopkins

D.6   W. H. Auden

D.7   Thom Gunn

D.8   Vernon Scannell

Index of Poets[1]

[1]Only the authors of complete poems are listed.

Index of First Lines[1]

[1]Only poems which appear in full are included.

Acknowledgements

Thanks are due to the following for kind permission to reprint the poems and prose included in this book:

W.H. Auden and Faber and Faber Ltd. for 'The Capital', 'Musée des Beaux Arts' and 'Lullaby' from *Collected Shorter Poems 1927–1957*; transcripts of 'The Tyger' by William Blake, courtesy of the British Museum; Tony Connor and the Oxford University Press for 'End of the World' from *With Love Somehow*; E. E. Cummings and Macgibbon and Kee Ltd. for 'go(perpe)go' from *Complete Poems*; Paul Dehn and Hamish Hamilton Ltd. for 'Explanation' from *Fern on the Rock*, copyright © 1965 by Paul Dehn (Hamish Hamilton, London); Emily Dickinson for 'I measure every Grief I meet', reprinted by permission of the publishers and the Trustees of Amherst College from Thomas H. Johnson, Editor, *The Poems of Emily Dickinson*, Cambridge, Mass.: The Belknap Press of Harvard University Press, Copyright, 1951, 1955, by The President and Fellows of Harvard College; Alfred Douglas and John Baker Publishers Limited for 'London' from *Sonnets*; T. S. Eliot and Faber and Faber Ltd. for 'Rhapsody on a Windy Night' from *Collected Poems*; D. J. Enright and David Higham Associates Ltd. for 'Blue Umbrellas' from *Bread Rather Than Blossoms*, published by Secker and Warburg Ltd.; John Freeman and A. D. Peters & Company for 'It Was the Lovely Moon' from *Collected Poems*, published by Macmillan & Co., Ltd.; Robert Frost and Laurence Pollinger Ltd. for 'Out, Out', 'The Silken Tent' and 'Fire and Ice' from *The Complete Poems of Robert Frost*, published by Jonathan Cape Limited; Thom Gunn and Faber and Faber Ltd. for 'Considering the Snail' from *My Sad Captains*, 'Tamer and Hawk' from *Fighting Terms* and 'First Meeting with a Possible Mother-in-Law' from *The Sense of Movement*; Robert Graves and A. P. Watt & Son for 'Conversation Piece' from *Collected Poems 1959*; Michael Hamburger for 'Paddington Canal' from *Flowering Cactus*; Trustees of the Hardy Estate and Macmillan & Co. Ltd. for 'Drummer Hodge', 'Neutral Tones', 'At Castle Boterel' and 'Snow in the Suburbs' from *The Collected Poems of Thomas Hardy*, and an extract from *The Mayor of Casterbridge* by Thomas Hardy; Seamus Heaney and Faber and Faber Ltd. for 'Scaffolding', 'Storm on the Island' and 'Twice Shy' from *Death of a Naturalist*; John Heath-Stubbs and David Higham Associates Ltd. for 'Now in My Hall' from *Selected Poems of John Heath-Stubbs*, published by Oxford University Press; H. G. Henderson and Doubleday & Company, Inc. for 'City People' from *An Introduction to Haiku* by Harold G. Henderson, copyright © 1958 by Harold G. Henderson, reprinted by permission of Doubleday & Company, Inc.; The Society of Authors, literary representative of the Estate of the late A. E. Housman, and Jonathan Cape Ltd., publishers of A. E. Housman's *Collected Poems*, for 'With Rue My Heart Is Laden' and 'Tell Me Not Here' from *Collected Poems*; Ted Hughes and Faber and Faber Ltd. for 'Wind' and 'The Thought Fox' from *The Hawk in The Rain* and 'A Woman Unconscious', 'Hawk Roosting' and 'To Paint a Waterlily' from *Lupercal*; James Kirkup for 'Wreathmakers in Leeds Marketplace' from *A Correct Compassion*, published by Oxford University Press; Philip Larkin and Faber and Faber Ltd. for 'Here' and 'Days' from *The Whitsun Weddings*, and 'Lines on a Young Lady's Photograph Album' by Philip Larkin, reprinted from *The Less Deceived* by permission of the Marvell Press, England; C. Day Lewis and Jonathan Cape Ltd. for 'Time to Go' from *Pegasus*; Laurence Pollinger Limited and the Estate of the late Mrs. Frieda Lawrence for 'Piano' and 'Bat' from *The Complete Poems of D. H. Lawrence*, published by William Heinemann Limited; Louis MacNeice and Faber and Faber Ltd. for 'Soap Suds', 'Slow Movement' and 'To the Public' from *Collected Poems*; Archibald MacLeish and The Bodley Head for 'The End of the World' from *Poems*; The Literary Trustees of Walter de la Mare and the Society of Authors as their representative for permission to reprint 4 lines from 'Railway Junction' and 'The Song of the Mad Prince' by Walter de la Mare; Christopher Middleton and Longmans Green & Co. Ltd. for 'The Thousand Things' from *Torse 3*; Ogden Nash and J. M. Dent & Sons Ltd. for 'Very Like a Whale' from *Many Long Years Ago* and 'Strange Case of the Lovelorn Letter Writer' from *The Private Dining Room*; Howard Nemerov and Laurence Pollinger Ltd, for 'Redeployment' from *Five American Poets*, published by Faber and Faber Ltd.; Harold Owen, the British Museum and Chatto and Windus Ltd. for permission to reproduce transcripts of manuscripts drafts of 'Anthem for Doomed Youth' by Wilfred Owen; Harold Owen and Chatto and Windus Ltd. for extracts from 'Exposure', 'Asleep' and 'Arms and the Boy' from *The Collected Poems of Wilfred Owen*; Peter Porter and Scorpion Press for 'Annotations of Auschwitz' from *Once Bitten Twice Bitten*; Ezra Pound and Faber and Faber Ltd. for 'In a Station of the Metro' from *Personae;* Peter Redgrove and Routledge & Kegan Paul Ltd. for '13 Ways of Looking at a Blackboard' from *The Collector and Other Poems*; Theodore Roethke and Martin Secker & Warburg Ltd. for 'Orchids' from *Words for the Wind*; Colin Rowbotham for 'Appointment'; Carl Sandburg and Holt, Rinehart & Winston Inc. for 'Fog' from *Chicago Poems*, published by Jonathan Cape Ltd.; George Sassoon for 'Does It Matter' and 'The Kiss' from *Collected Poems of Siegfried Sassoon*; Vernon Scannell for 'The Men Who Wear My Clothes'; Louis Simpson and Wesleyan University Press for 'Carentan O Carentan', copyright © 1959 by Louis Simpson, reprinted from *A Dream of Governors*, by Louis Simpson, by permission of Wesleyan University Press; Edith Sitwell and Gerald Duckworth & Co. Ltd. for 'When Sir Beelzebub' from *Facade and Other Poems 1920–1935* by Edith Sitwell; Stephen Spender and Faber and Faber Ltd. for 'The Pylons' from *Collected Poems*; Stanley Snaith and Jonathan Cape Ltd. for 'To Some Builders of Cities' from *Green Legacy*; Mrs. O. Soyinka for permission to reprint 'Telephone Conversation' by Wole Soyinka from *Reflections*, edited by Francis Ademola and published by African Universities Press Ltd., 1962; L. A. G. Strong and Methuen & Co. Ltd. for 'Winter' from *The Body's Imperfections*; Trustees for the Copyrights of the late Dylan Thomas for 'Poem on his Birthday' (and four worksheets of poem), 'In My Craft or Sullen Art' and 'And Death Shall Have no Dominion' from *Collected Poems of Dylan Thomas*, published by J. M. Dent & Sons Ltd.; R. S. Thomas and Rupert Hart-Davis Ltd. for 'An Old Man' from *Song at the Year's Turning*, 'A Blackbird Singing' from *Poetry for Supper* and 'Here' and 'Walter Llywarch' from *Tares*; Charles Tomlinson for extract

231

from 'How Still the Hawk' from *Seeing is Believing*, by Charles Tomlinson, by permission of the Oxford University Press; Michael Yeats and Macmillan & Co. Ltd. for 'Wild Swans at Coole' and 'When You Are Old And Grey' from *Collected Poems* by W. B. Yeats.

Every effort has been made to trace the copyright owner of the late D. Capetanakis's 'Abel' from *Capetanakis—A Greek Poet in England*.